LAW
ENFORCEMENT
AGENCIES

SWAT TEAMS

LAW ENFORCEMENT AGENCIES

Bomb Squad

Border Patrol

Federal Bureau of Investigation

The Secret Service

SWAT Teams

The Texas Rangers

LAW ENFORCEMENT AGENCIES

SWAT TEAMS

Michael Newton

CHELSEA HOUSE PUBLISHERS
An imprint of Infobase Publishing

SWAT TEAMS

Chelsea House
An imprint of Infobase Publishing
132 West 31st Street
New York NY 10001

Library of Congress Cataloging-in-Publication Data

Newton, Michael, 1951-
SWAT teams / Michael Newton.
p. cm. — (Law enforcement agencies)
Includes bibliographical references and index.
ISBN-13: 978-1-60413-625-8 (hbk. : alk. paper)
ISBN-10: 1-60413-625-1 (hbk. : alk. paper)
1. Police—Special weapons and tactics units—Juvenile literature. I. Title. II. Series.
HV8080.S64N49 2010
363.2′32—dc22   2010026511

Chelsea House books are available at special discounts when purchased in bulk quantities for businesses, associations, institutions, or sales promotions. Please call our Special Sales Department in New York at (212) 967-8800 or (800) 322-8755.

You can find Chelsea House on the World Wide Web at http://www.chelseahouse.com

Text design and composition by Erika K. Arroyo
Cover design by Keith Trego
Cover printed by Bang Printing, Brainerd, Minn.
Book printed and bound by Bang Printing, Brainerd, Minn.
Date printed: November 2010

Printed in the United States of America

10 9 8 7 6 5 4 3 2 1

This book is printed on acid-free paper.

All links and Web addresses were checked and verified to be correct at the time of publication. Because of the dynamic nature of the Web, some addresses and links may have changed since publication and may no longer be valid.

Contents

Introduction

Law enforcement is dangerous business. While it does not rank among America's 10 most dangerous occupations—fishermen, pilots, loggers, construction workers, and farmers all suffer higher on-the-job death rates[1]—only soldiers in combat face a greater risk of being killed deliberately by other human beings.

Between January 1791 and February 2009, at least 19,379 American law enforcement officers died from injuries or illness suffered in the line of duty. Sixty-three percent of those (12,212) lost their lives as a direct result of violent action-shooting, stabbing, bombing, or assault-by criminals whom they were trying to arrest.[2]

Most law enforcement is reactive, a response to some report of criminal activity. Police are governed by specific state and federal laws, and their response to crime is limited by funding from the government. Historically, police have lagged behind lawbreakers in adopting new technology, from cars and aircraft to radio communications, modern weapons, and computers. They are always outnumbered, and often outgunned.

In times of crisis, law enforcement must adapt more quickly than in peaceful periods, when crime rates drop and public safety seems secure. Such crises commonly occur in wartime, during economic hardship, and in times of social or political upheaval, when dissent turns violent and governments feel threatened by rebellion.

In the Great Depression of the 1930s, record unemployment set millions of Americans adrift in search of jobs or government relief checks, while gangs of outlaws looted banks and kidnapped wealthy individuals for ransom. In the midst of that "crime wave," new laws were passed permitting federal agents to chase fugitives across state lines, while local police armed themselves with machine guns and bulletproof vehicles. Crimes formerly punished by state courts alone—such as bank robbery and kidnapping—became federal offenses, vastly expanding the U.S. government's authority.

Decades later, in the late 1960s and early 1970s, police confronted a new type of challenge. America's civil rights movement shifted from nonviolent civil disobedience toward militant action, while student unrest and fierce resistance to the war in Vietnam produced a wave of violent attacks on government and industry, the military, and police. At the same time, members of foreign radical groups carried their fight to American soil from Europe, the Middle East, and Latin America. Riots, bombings, and airline hijackings demanded a swift and decisive response from law enforcement nationwide and around the world.

From that era of crisis emerged police and military special response teams, broadly lumped together since 1967 under the label of "SWAT"— *Special Weapons and Tactics*. As the units grew and spread, earning their reputation on the streets, Hollywood stepped in to glamorize, distort, and sometimes even demonize the officers who place themselves in harm's way on a daily basis. From NBC's *S.W.A.T.* series (1975–76) set in a fictitious Southern California town, to director Clark Johnson's violent feature film of the same title in 2003, SWAT officers have blazed their way through people's imaginations and media headlines.

But what is the truth?

SWAT Teams answers that question, examining the history, techniques, successes, and failures of police special response units worldwide. The book consists of eight chapters.

Chapter 1, "What Is SWAT?," describes the organization, duties, and training techniques of a modern SWAT team.

Chapter 2, "SWAT History," surveys the history of police special response units from 1930 to the formal birth of SWAT teams in the mid-1960s and beyond, through their expansion worldwide.

Chapter 3, "LAPD SWAT," reviews the history of America's first recognized SWAT team, organized by the Los Angeles Police Department (LAPD) in 1967.

Chapter 4, "Federal SWAT Teams," charts the birth and evolution of the first federal SWAT team, organized by the Federal Bureau of Investigation (FBI) in 1983.

Chapter 5, "Special Weapons and Tactics," examines the tools, vehicles, and methods that gave SWAT its name, while enabling officers to save lives and capture felons in extraordinary circumstances.

Chapter 6, "Hostage Negotiation," details techniques employed in the most delicate of SWAT duties: freeing hostages without injury to them or their kidnappers.

Chapter 7, "Controversial Cases," discusses cases in which SWAT operations have sparked controversy and claims of excessive, unjustified force.

Chapter 8, "SWAT International," circles the globe to visit foreign SWAT teams in action.

What Is SWAT?

Columbine, Colorado

High school was hard on 18-year-old seniors Eric Harris and Dylan Klebold, a pair of outsiders who spent most of their free time target shooting, customizing violent video games, and writing angry online blogs about the bullying they suffered at Columbine High School. In January 1998 they faced criminal charges for breaking into a locked van, but both made good impressions on juvenile officers from the Jefferson County Sheriff's Department, negotiating terms of community service and psychiatric counseling in lieu of confinement. The boys were so polite to their probation officer that he released them from supervision ahead of schedule.

In March 1998 a Columbine classmate's parents complained to police that Harris had threatened their son on his Web site, after a quarrel at school. Officers drafted a warrant request to search Harris's home for weapons, but for reasons still unclear, the paperwork was never filed and no search was conducted. Meanwhile, Harris and Klebold had obtained four guns, including two shotguns with barrels sawed off (in violation of federal law), and they were busy building homemade bombs.

At 11:10 A.M. on April 20, 1999, Harris and Klebold arrived at Columbine High, placing duffel bags filled with explosive devices inside the school cafeteria. The charges were set to blow at 11:17, causing a panic in the school that would allow Harris and Klebold to shoot students and teachers on the run, as they fled the building. When the bombs failed to explode, the boys invaded Columbine High with their guns and more bombs at 11:19 and began shooting people at random. Over the next 49 minutes, they killed one teacher and a dozen students, wounded 23 other victims, set fires, and detonated several crude pipe bombs.

The first sheriff's deputy reached Columbine High at 11:24 A.M. and radioed for assistance. One minute later, the sheriff's office received its first 911 emergency call from the school, with gunshots audible over the phone. County SWAT team members scrambled to respond, but it was already too late for some of Harris and Klebold's victims. Officers had the school surrounded by the time both gunmen shot themselves in the campus library at 12:08 P.M., but no one on the outside knew that they were dead.

The first SWAT officers entered Columbine High School at 1:09 P.M., alert to danger and expecting gunfire, but all they found were terrified and wounded victims. Student Patrick Ireland, shot four times, escaped through a library window at 2:38 and was caught on camera as SWAT team members helped him to safety. It was 3:30 P.M. when police found Harris and Klebold dead in the library, and another hour passed before the school was cleared. Even then, the danger had not passed; officers found another bomb in Klebold's car at 6:15 P.M. It detonated at 10:45 as they tried to defuse it, but no one was injured. Bomb squad officers swept the high school on April 21, before the final 13 bodies were removed.

Ten days after the massacre, on April 30, Jefferson County officials convened a secret meeting to discuss the fact that sheriff's officer Michael Guerra and others had known of Eric Harris's threatening Web site 13 months prior to the Columbine shootings. They voted to conceal that information, and the fact was not revealed until September 2001, prompting angry charges of official negligence.[1] Outsiders also criticized the county's SWAT team for failing to enter the school building sooner, a judgment that team members on the scene regarded as unfair.

WHEN DUTY CALLS

Most SWAT team deployments do not involve full-scale massacres such as the Columbine incident, but officers assigned to police special

Members of a SWAT team march to Columbine High School in Littleton, Colorado, as they prepare to do a final search of the school. (*AP Photo/Ed Andrieski, File*)

response units are trained to cope effectively with a variety of high-risk situations. Normal SWAT duties include the following:

- Apprehending barricaded subjects, whether in their homes or a commercial setting, armed or otherwise
- Hostage rescue, whenever victims are held captive and threatened by criminals
- Rescue of officers or civilians wounded or trapped in shooting situations
- Stabilizing crises involving suicidal subjects

- Counterterrorist operations in urban or rural settings
- Assistance with dangerous missions, including raids, searches, and arrests of violent gang members, rapists, and serial killers
- Conducting manhunts for dangerous subjects at large after shootings, armed robberies, and other violent crimes
- Mobile assaults on moving vehicles, including boats, buses, and trains
- Airborne operations, typically aerial assaults from helicopters

THE McDONALD'S MASSACRE (1984)

James Oliver Huberty (1942–84) was an Ohio native with a long history of violent behavior, including repeated assaults on his wife and threats toward his neighbors. To make things worse, a motorcycle accident left Huberty with brain damage and a persistent twitching in one arm that cost him his job as a welder. In January 1984 Huberty moved his family to San Diego, California, and found work as a security guard, but his poor attitude got him fired in July. One week later, on July 18, Huberty left home with three guns, telling his wife, "Society had its chance. I'm going hunting—hunting humans." Despite his record and the three guns, Huberty's wife failed to contact police.

From home, Huberty walked to a nearby McDonald's restaurant, pulled one of his guns, and ordered the people inside to lie down on the floor. Although he had never served in the military, Huberty told his hostages, "I killed thousands in Vietnam and I'll kill thousands more!" He then opened fire on the captives, switching between an Uzi semiautomatic carbine, a 12-gauge shotgun, and a 9mm pistol, and pausing to reload as he emptied the guns. In addition to restaurant patrons and employees, Huberty also shot an elderly couple walking past the restaurant and two boys riding bicycles outside.

The first emergency report sent police racing to the wrong McDonald's location, but further calls redirected them to the

- Assistance with special military operations, as in riot zones or following declaration of martial law
- Protection of public figures, including provision of security against long-range snipers
- Providing additional security at special events, such as the Olympics, where dangerous criminal or terrorist activity is expected
- General crime suppression, as when SWAT joins in periodic street sweeps of high-crime urban areas

massacre scene. SWAT team hostage negotiators tried to communicate with Huberty, but he ignored them. Two snipers were posted outside the restaurant, one atop an apartment building, the other—Officer Chuck Foster—on the roof of a doughnut shop. One hour and 17 minutes after Huberty started shooting, Foster fired a single shot and killed the gunman instantly, striking his heart and spine.

The scene was grim. San Diego Chief of Police Bill Kolender called it "a sickening massacre," telling reporters, "It's the most terrible thing I've ever seen in my life, and I've been in the business 28 years."[2] Huberty had fired 257 shots, killing 21 victims and wounding 19 more.The dead ranged in age from eight months to 74 years, and included a pregnant woman gunned down with her infant son. If not for Officer Foster, the toll might have been much worse.

Two months after the massacre, McDonald's demolished the restaurant and donated its land to the city. In 1988 the site became an off-campus education center affiliated with Southwestern Community College. A monument consisting of 21 granite pillars, ranging in height from one to six feet, commemorates the victims. Huberty's widow sued McDonald's and her husband's ex-employer for $5 million, claiming that his violent behavior was triggered by junk food and factory pollutants, but she later dropped the case on advice from her attorney.[3]

Despite the reckless behavior sometimes portrayed in fiction and film, SWAT officers are expected to accomplish all of these demanding tasks—and more—without unnecessary loss of life, injury, or damage to personal property. Successful missions are those in which *no one* is harmed, on either side of the law.

READY FOR ACTION

While SWAT officers stand ready to respond at a moment's notice in crisis situations, most law enforcement agencies also require them to perform normal police duties. Few police departments are large or rich enough to leave SWAT teams sitting around at headquarters, cleaning guns or working out in the gym while they wait for emergency calls. Instead, they typically serve normal roles as patrol officers or detectives until they are summoned by radio, cell phone, or pager to answer an emergency call. Special clothing and equipment is hidden in their duty vehicles or carried to the crisis scene in special vans; SWAT members spend most of each shift in standard uniforms or plain clothes.

But the call to action may come at any time.

During 2001–03, for example, LAPD SWAT teams responded to 542 call-outs, an average of 3.5 alerts per week. Of those alarms, 332 involved barricaded subjects, while 210 required service of high-risk warrants.[4] Smaller departments in low-crime communities may not deploy their SWAT teams once in any given year—assuming they *have* a SWAT team—but lulls in the action provide time for more attention to training and organization.

SWAT teams are normally organized on a "building block" pattern, with an overall commander supervising specific units. In a large department, such as LAPD, the New York City Police Department (NYPD), or the FBI, SWAT responsibilities are commonly divided among perimeter teams (responsible for securing a crime scene's boundaries against intruders or escaping fugitives), sniper/observer teams (in charge of long-range marksmanship), entry/arrest teams (which penetrate objectives to serve warrants and arrest suspects), and hostage negotiators.[5] Smaller departments may not have the personnel available to specialize, but any SWAT team worthy of the name includes at least one sniper and an entry/arrest squad.

Aside from dignitary protection and patrols at special events, most SWAT team missions are either emergency call-outs or service of high-risk warrants. The first group includes all unexpected situations: threatened suicides, barricaded subjects (with or without hostages), and shootings (whether officer-involved or otherwise). Since no advance warning is given, police must play catch-up with the criminals involved, normally arriving on the scene with no clear idea of a building's floor plan, the number of felons and victims inside, or the weapons which they will face. Summoned from routine duties—or, perhaps, from home—they must rely on training, personal experience, and any information they can gather at the scene.

Warrant service, while equally urgent in the case of violent felons and potentially explosive situations (such as criminal drug labs), commonly allows for greater preparation. Officers know in advance where they are going and whom they plan to arrest, although others may also be present without the team's knowledge. Teams often have street maps and floor plans available for strategic planning. In some cases, if time permits, a SWAT team may even rehearse its entry to a specific target, using officers in place of subjects for the simulation. Ideally, there is time to isolate the target and evacuate neighbors, if substantial danger is anticipated.[6]

SELECTION AND TRAINING

While fictional portrayals make SWAT team duty attractive to thrill-seekers, much as *The Silence of the Lambs* produced a glut of applications for psychological profiling jobs with the FBI, SWAT is not open to all applicants. The job's physical and emotional demands dictate rigorous selection standards and strict—even harsh—training methods to keep those finally chosen in top fighting form.

For starters, no civilian off the street can simply join a SWAT team. Those selected to serve on special response units must be veteran law enforcement officers and possess special qualities beyond the norm for "average" police. Some units—including the FBI's Hostage Rescue Team—prefer SWAT applicants with military backgrounds above and beyond police service, especially those who have served with elite

(Continues on page 20)

SUICIDE BY COP

"Suicide by cop"—or victim-precipitated homicide—is a phenomenon involving subjects who crave death but lack the will to kill themselves. Whether intoxicated, mentally disturbed, or simply mindful of suicide clauses restricting life-insurance payments, such individuals provoke confrontations with police in hopes of being shot. Sometimes they wield toy guns, unloaded weapons, or make-believe "bombs" to encourage a shooting, often while threatening hostages.

Psychologists recognize various potential warning signs of an impending "suicide by cop."[7] They include a subject who

★ has a record of assaults or other violent crimes.
★ has killed someone, particularly a close friend or relative.
★ is barricaded and refuses to negotiate.
★ declares that "You'll never take me alive."
★ announces that he has a life-threatening illness.
★ admits suicidal thoughts or plans.
★ has recently suffered traumatic life-changing events.
★ does not include negotiation of escape in his demands.
★ has given away his money and possessions before the standoff.
★ has expressed a wish to die in a "big" or "macho" way.
★ expresses feelings of hopelessness.
★ sets unreasonable terms or deadlines for conclusion of the standoff.
★ dictates his last will and testament to police negotiators.
★ demands to be killed by police.

Police Sergeant Richard Parent, in his 2004 doctoral thesis at Simon Fraser University's School of Criminology at Burnaby, British Columbia, surveyed 843 fatal police shootings and determined that roughly 50 percent were victim-precipitated homicides.[8] A few examples include the following:

★ *January 2005:* Andres Reya, a member of the U.S. Marine Corps, chose to shoot it out with SWAT team members in

Ceres, California, rather than serve a second tour of combat duty in Iraq. Reya killed Sergeant Howard Stevenson and wounded Officer Sam Ryno before other SWAT officers shot and killed him.

★ *February 2005:* Intoxicated subject William Henkle attacked police with a chainsaw at his home in Wilkes-Barre, Pennsylvania, and was shot 13 times before he collapsed. Autopsy tests revealed blood-alcohol levels six times the state's legal limit for operating a motor vehicle.

★ *May 2005:* Following a violent quarrel with his pregnant wife at their home in Orlando, Florida, Alberto Rodriguez-Sobrino declared, "I know somebody is going to die today, and I know that is going to be me."[9] When police arrived, summoned by his wife, Rodriguez-Sobrino attacked them with a knife and was shot down.

★ *July 2005:* SWAT officers surrounded the Los Angeles home of Jose Peña at 3:45 P.M., after he threatened relatives with a pistol. Peña emerged from the house at 5:30, carrying the gun and his 19-month-old daughter Suzie. He fired several shots at police, who returned fire, killing Peña and the child. As LAPD Lieutenant Paul Vernon told reporters, "When officers fired in self-defense, the suspect went down, as well as the baby." Facing harsh criticism from community activists, LAPD Chief William Bratton described Peña as "a cold-blooded killer," though in fact he had killed no one.[10]

★ *January 2006:* Christopher Penley, a 15-year-old student at Milwee Middle School in Longwood, Florida, held a classmate hostage at gunpoint in an outdoor restroom after the other boy glimpsed Penley's pistol. The hostage soon escaped, and police were summoned to the campus. After a 20-minute standoff, Penley emerged and aimed his pistol at officers, who shot and killed him. Sheriff Don Eslinger told reporters that Penley was "suicidal," first aiming his gun at himself and stating his plan to "die one way or another," before he pointed the weapon at police.[11]

(Continued from page 17)

units such as the Navy SEALs, Army Special Forces ("Green Berets"), or Marine Corps Force Reconnaissance companies. At the very least, SWAT applicants must be in top physical condition, capable of meeting challenges beyond those normally encountered in police academy training for patrol officers, and must excel in marksmanship with a variety of weapons. Psychological tests weed out those who seek a SWAT position based on some vague desire for adventure or an attraction to violence.

Once accepted as an applicant, SWAT recruits enter a period of training that never ends as long as they serve with the team. Preliminary qualification is only the first hurdle, screening out those applicants who cannot "cut it" as individuals, while advanced training tests the ability to perform as part of a team in life-or-death encounters. Beyond

A Louisiana SWAT team participates in a mock hostage situation training exercise. The "hostages" are played by Louisiana college students. (*AP Photo/*The Town Talk, *Abbey Brown)*

physical conditioning, detailed instruction in the use and maintenance of specialized equipment couples with classes on legal procedure (search and seizure, use of deadly force, etc.), first-aid, rappelling and climbing techniques, handling of hazardous materials, and use of weapons normally not issued to officers on routine patrol or investigations (explosives, "flash-bang" stun grenades, sniper rifles, etc.).

Beyond preliminary training lies probation, a period when rookie SWAT team members prove themselves—or fail—on real-life call-outs with their team. New officers, while highly trained and tested, still must prove themselves in action against desperate felons who follow no script, and whose weapons are loaded with deadly live rounds. Probationary supervision of officers on routine patrol commonly ranges from six months to two years, depending on the given agency's rules. Probation for a SWAT rookie may be judged by on-the-job experience and extended if the team is rarely mobilized. Probationary status may be reimposed on veterans if they make critical mistakes during a call-out.

Sergeant Joe Balicki, with the Orange County (California) Sheriff's Department SWAT team, described the standard applicant-screening process in April 2008. "You need to think on your feet, be able to handle specialized weapons, and make split second decisions," he said. "If you are in good shape now, you have to stay in good shape. Attitude, arrogance will not be tolerated. Whether a new SWAT member comes for a humble assignment or an elite investigations billet, doesn't matter. We have guys who come from Special Investigations or other high profile details, [but] it doesn't matter here. Here you are the new guy on the team. We have an image to maintain on and off duty. If you can't handle yourself off duty or you make us look bad, it will not be tolerated."[12]

Basic entrance testing for the Orange County SWAT team includes a minimum of 15 pull-ups, timed negotiation of an obstacle course while wearing a 30-pound tactical vest, rappelling from a 60-foot tower with no fear of heights, and crawling through narrow tunnels without claustrophobia. "You don't have to like it," Sgt. Balicki noted, "you just have to be able to do it." Next comes a test of marksmanship with varied weapons, at ranges between five and 25 yards. As Sgt. Balicki observes, top marksmanship is essential. "It's not just physical fitness," he explains. "The applicants have to know how to handle weapons. We're the Special Weapons and Tactics Team, not the running team."[13]

In exchange for the added risks and responsibility of service on a special response unit, SWAT team members generally receive no additional salary. Some departments, which require SWAT officers to buy their own equipment, add a stipend to their paychecks, but it rarely covers the expenses of the job. Special training required for maintenance of SWAT team status, in many cases, must be performed on the officer's own time, without overtime pay. In most police departments, pay raises come through time on the job or advancement in rank rather than through voluntary assumption of extra duties.

And SWAT team members should expect to be disturbed at any hour of the day or night. Orange County's Sargeant Balicki explains, "You'll be called at all crappy hours. Saturday night at 1 A.M. and 3 A.M. are the favorite times to call us." For that reason, he says, recruits with stable home lives are preferred.[14]

SWAT History

Pittsburgh, Pennsylvania

At 2:00 A.M. on January 8, 2009, police visited the North Point Breeze apartments in search of a female tenant. The woman's father had called to complain of threats against his daughter from her boyfriend, Lamar Smith, whose criminal record included convictions for assault, robbery, drug and firearms violations, and intimidating a witness. Smith also faced an outstanding arrest warrant for drunken driving.

When officers arrived, they found Smith sitting outside his girl-friend's apartment, holding a pistol in each hand. When ordered to drop the guns, he bolted inside and slammed the apartment door behind him. Police headquarters dispatched a SWAT team and three hostage negotiators to the scene for what became a nine-hour siege. During the standoff, Smith played blaring music and shouted at police, saying, "I'm gonna die! I'm gonna die!"[1]

At one point, after firing a shot inside his apartment, Smith tried to escape through a window. SWAT officers knocked him back inside with a nonlethal "beanbag" projectile and then launched canisters of pepper spray into the dwelling. Speaking to negotiators by phone, Smith twice agreed to surrender, then twice changed his mind. Finally, when he broke off communication at noon, SWAT officers stormed the apartment.

Smith met them inside, still armed with two pistols, advancing as the officers came through his door. The entry team again demanded his surrender, but Smith kept his pistols raised until a SWAT sniper fired through the window, killing Smith where he stood.

Opinions on the shooting were divided. Smith's uncle told reporters, "They wouldn't let us in to talk to him, to end it peacefully. The police killed him because of a domestic dispute, because of nothing." Pittsburgh Police Chief Nate Harper explained that SWAT does not permit civilians to enter standoff situations where they may become victims or hostages. "The [SWAT sniper's] actions were justified because the suspect did approach the officers with weapons in both hands after a nine-hour ordeal," Harper said. "It was an unfortunate incident that occurred. Our condolences go out to the suspect's family."[2]

Pullman, Washington

Members of the Phi Kappa Sigma fraternity chapter at Washington State University were placed on probation in summer 2008 for violations of the school's drinking code. Despite this disciplinary action, problems persisted, and at 8:30 P.M. on January 21, 2009, police received reports of a drunken party in progress at the frat house. A patrolman arrived, observed intoxicated students playing with "airsoft" pellet guns on the lawn, and saw a bag of marijuana in a car parked outside. The officer radioed headquarters, where supervisors obtained search warrants for the frat house and the vehicle.

Shortly before midnight, a SWAT team arrived on the scene, consisting of officers drawn from the Pullman Police Department, the Whitman County Sheriff's Office, and the Washington State University Police Department. They raided the frat house, seized "misdemeanor levels" of marijuana and drug paraphernalia, and while no actual arrests were made, one fraternity member received a citation for obstructing police.[3]

Students and some outside observers denounced the call-out of a SWAT team to break up a noisy party. J.D. Tuccille, writing for Denver's *Civil Liberties Examiner*, complained that "calling in the heavy weapons to address that particular legal transgression is a major overreaction," adding that "SWAT teams and enforcement of laws against nonviolent activities are two things that don't go so well together. Unless, that is, you think downing a beer a few months before your 21st birthday should carry the death penalty."[4]

Pullman Police Department Commander Chris Tennant responded by telling reporters that local law enforcement agencies were simply short-handed. "We activated the SWAT team not because we needed special weapons and tactics," Tennant said. "We just needed the bodies."[5]

Wichita Falls, Texas

At 12:15 A.M. on February 2, 2009, a frantic caller dialed 911 in Wichita Falls, reporting that a man had dragged a struggling woman into a house on the city's south side. The first police officer on the scene peered through a window, observing a man armed with a shotgun and a pistol. His report scrambled a SWAT team, which surrounded the house and called for those inside to come out empty-handed.

A tense standoff ensued, with hostage negotiators making several attempts to contact the home's occupants. The siege ended peacefully when three males and a woman emerged from the house with hands raised. Inside the dwelling, SWAT officers found the two guns, plus a "large amount" of marijuana. The woman was released after a medical examination found no injuries; she declined to press charges. Officers held the male subjects, ranging in age from 17 to 23, on Class A misdemeanor charges of possessing marijuana in excess of two ounces. If convicted, they faced a maximum penalty of one year in jail and a $4,000 fine.[6]

SWAT GENESIS

The three aforementioned incidents, all occurring within a four-week span, indicate the broad range of duties assigned to SWAT teams—and the split-second choices involved that may produce triumph or tragedy. Police work is diverse and dangerous. A routine traffic stop or a domestic argument may end in violence, while panicked calls of bloody murder in progress may prove to be a false alarm. Police cannot predict what waits for them until they reach the scene, and SWAT stands ready to assist if patrol officers find themselves overwhelmed.

Published reports often credit LAPD with the creation of the first SWAT team, but that is not the case. New York City launched its Emergency Service Division as a riot-control team in April 1930, evolving by the 1960s into a combination of a SWAT team, bomb squad, and all-purpose rescue unit (renamed the Emergency Service Unit).[7] The first dedicated SWAT team, as we recognize them today, was the Toronto Police Department's Emergency Task Force, created in 1965 and best known since 2008 for its depiction in the television series *Flashpoint*.

ANTHONY KIRITSIS

Indianapolis, Indiana, resident Anthony Kiritsis fell behind on his mortgage payments in 1976 and became enraged when banker Richard Hall refused to extend his deadline. Convinced that Hall wanted the land for himself, Kiritsis invaded Hall's office on February 8, 1977, armed with a pistol and a sawed-off shotgun. After scuffling with Hall, Kiritsis wired the shotgun to Hall's neck with a "dead man's line," designed to fire if Kiritsis released the weapon. When the first police arrived, Kiritsis shouted to them, "If you shoot me, he's a goner!"[8]

Thus began a 63-hour ordeal, during which Kiritsis marched Hall from his office, commandeered a police car, and drove to an apartment Kiritsis had rented. SWAT officers followed, troubled by reports that Kiritsis had recently purchased 50 pounds of dynamite. From his apartment, Kiritsis made a series of phone calls to a local radio station, demanding money, an apology from his mortgage company, and immunity from prosecution. A hostage negotiator stalled for time, finally producing a lawyer from the mortgage company who promised Kiritsis $5 million and legal immunity.

The standoff ended with a rambling televised speech by Kiritsis. Finally satisfied, Kiritsis unfastened the shotgun from Hall's neck, then fired a blast as proof it was loaded. Despite the attorney's false promise, police charged Kiritsis with kidnapping. Jurors later acquitted him on grounds of insanity, whereupon Kiritsis was committed to a mental institution. Released in January 1988 over objections from authorities, Kiritsis retreated into obscurity and died in January 2005, at age 72.

In the United States, meanwhile, it took dissent and tragedy to motivate refinement of police special response units.

Police in Delano, California, created a SWAT team of sorts in 1965, after the United Farm Workers union led a strike against local grape growers. Violence resulted, most of which was caused by strikebreakers, which prompted Delano police commanders to train their officers for crowd control and counter-sniper tactics.[9] Los Angeles police noted Delano's efforts, but they put action on hold until a grisly mass-murder shocked America and the world.

SNIPER!

Charles Whitman was a Florida native, born in 1941, who followed a childhood obsession with guns into the U.S. Marine Corps at age 18. While still in uniform, he won a military scholarship to study mechanical engineering at the University of Texas in Austin. There, he met and married fellow student Kathleen Leissner, but his love of guns and hunting soon got Whitman in trouble. In 1963 he shot a deer and skinned it in his dormitory room, resulting in the loss of his scholarship.

Returning to active military duty, Whitman was court-martialed in November 1964 for gambling, possessing a personal firearm on base, and threatening another Marine over a debt. Upon conviction, Whitman served 30 days in the brig (a place of confinement or detention, especially in the U.S. Navy or Marines) and 90 days of hard labor. Despite that incident, he received an honorable discharge in December 1964 and returned to the University of Texas to study architectural engineering.

Poor health sabotaged Whitman's attempt to build a new life. In March 1966 a campus doctor referred Whitman to psychiatrist Maurice Heatly, who found him "oozing with hostility," speaking of urges to climb the university's clock tower and "start shooting people with a deer rifle."[10] Whitman's diary also described incidents of domestic violence against Kathleen. The diary also reflected Whitman's resolve to become a better husband, but it was not to be.

On the night of July 31, 1966, Whitman fatally stabbed both his mother and wife, at their separate homes, leaving a suicide note with each victim. Early the next morning, he drove to the university campus with an arsenal that included two high-powered rifles, an M1 carbine, a sawed-off shotgun, and three pistols. Using his student ID, Whitman gained admittance to the school's clock tower and climbed 307 feet to its top.

He started shooting at 11:48 A.M., selecting random targets. Whitman's chosen weapons let him strike far and wide from the tower, killing 14 strangers and wounding 32 others while police scrambled to respond.[11] No tactical unit existed to deal with snipers, but officers did their best. A police sharpshooter, Lieutenant Marion Lee, commandeered a small private plane to stop Whitman, but he retreated after rifle shots punctured the aircraft.

Finally, Austin police officer Ramiro Martinez entered the tower, breaking through a door barricaded by Whitman. Two other Austin officers, Jerry Day and Houston McCoy, trailed Martinez with an armed civilian, Allen Crum. As Martinez approached the sniper's roost, Crum accidentally fired a shot from his rifle, alerting Whitman. While Whitman was distracted, Officer Martinez shot him twice with a 12-gauge shotgun from 50 feet away, ending the bloody siege.

This diagram, created in 1966, shows one portion of the tower from which Charles Whitman shot pedestrians on the Austin, Texas, streets below. He fired in several directions from the tower, killing 15 persons before he was slain by police. (*Hulton-Deutsch Collection/Corbis*)

Police seized the weapons used by Charles Whitman after they gunned him down in his perch in the University of Texas administration building tower. The incident helped to demonstrate the need for greater police preparation for emergency situations. (*AP Photo*)

At the time, Whitman's rampage was the worst American mass-murder since 1927, when deranged bomber Andrew Kehoe killed 45 persons and wounded 58 in Bath Township, Michigan.[12] The Texas slaughter came less than three weeks after sexual predator Richard Speck murdered eight student nurses in Chicago. Those crimes made headlines worldwide, with cover stories in *Life* magazine—and they convinced American police that greater preparation was required for such emergencies.

SELLING SWAT

In 1967 Publicity surrounded the LAPD's creation of the first special response team to use the "SWAT" designation, and similar units soon multiplied from coast to coast. While no comprehensive figures are available, published estimates claim that by 2005 American SWAT teams were mobilized for an average 40,000 call-outs per year.[13]

Special response teams, with or without the "SWAT" label, exist at seven different levels of law enforcement (excluding branches of the U.S. military, each of which maintains its own elite units). The first American SWAT teams, still the most common, are found within municipal (city or town) police departments. In 2000 the U.S. Census Bureau found approximately 30,000 incorporated municipalities nationwide, many with their own SWAT teams, ranging in size from those of the LAPD and NYPD to the Seymour (Connecticut) Police Department's Emergency Service Unit (population 15,000), the Eufaula (Alabama) Police Department's Tactical Team (14,000), and the Forest (Mississippi) Police Department's Direct Action Response Team (6,000).[14]

Even smaller towns—such as Butler, Missouri (population 4,201), Mt. Orab, Utah (2,701), and Middleburg, Pennsylvania (1,363)—also have SWAT teams, though their crime rates might not seem to justify the cost. In some cases, it seems that forming a SWAT team involves ego more than actual need. Lynn Haven, Florida (population 12,451), created a SWAT unit based on reports that local armed robberies had increased by 900 percent—but, as noted in the *St. Petersburg Times,* politicians acted "without telling regulators that the raw number of robberies rose from one to 10, then fell to one again just as quickly." By 1996, 65 percent of all American cities with populations between 25,000 and 50,000 had active SWAT teams, while 8 percent of the remainder in that range planned to start one.[15]

Another group of SWAT teams at the local level are maintained by non-municipal police departments, which patrol public facilities such as schools, airports, railroad terminals, and housing projects. Some of those units include San Francisco's Bay Area Rapid Transit District Police Department SWAT Team; the Los Angeles Airport Police Emergency Services Unit at L.A. International Airport; Florida's Miami-Dade Schools Police Department SWAT Team; the Antelope Valley College District Police Department Emergency Response Team in Lancaster, California; the Port Authority Police Department Emergency Services Unit operating in New York and New Jersey; the University of

Massachusetts Police Department Special Operations Unit; and the Ohio University Police Department SWAT Team.

The next-highest level of American law enforcement involves county authorities, usually (but not always) commanded by an officer known as the sheriff. The 50 states presently encompass 3,147 counties, called boroughs in Alaska, and parishes in Louisiana. Most county sheriff's departments include some kind of special response unit, known by various names. Non-SWAT titles include Wisconsin's Dane County Sheriff's Office Tactical Response Team, North Carolina's Gaston County Police Department Emergency Response Team, Georgia's Cobb County Sheriff's Office Tactical Operations Unit, and California's Los Angeles County Sheriff's Department Special Enforcement Detail.

When financial limitations prevent local police departments from creating individual SWAT teams, several agencies may join forces to create a regional team. Examples include the Central New Hampshire Special Operations Unit and the Belknap Regional Special Operations Group (covering New Hampshire's Lakes Region); the Grand Forks Regional SWAT Team (including members of four agencies in northwestern Minnesota and northeastern North Dakota); the Red River Valley SWAT Team (drawing officers from five departments in eastern North Dakota and western Minnesota); Metro Special Weapons and Tactics (with members from nine agencies in Pierce County, Washington); California's South Orange County Agencies Response Team; and MAMA-DERT—the *Multi-Agency Mutual Aid Drug Enforcement Response Team*—combining officers from six North Carolina counties with agents of the FBI and the Drug Enforcement Administration (DEA).

Next up the ladder of U.S. law enforcement, state police agencies in all 50 states maintain SWAT teams under various titles. They include the California Highway Patrol Special Weapons and Tactics Teams, Connecticut State Police Emergency Services Unit Tactical Team, Illinois State Police Tactical Response Team, the Louisiana Division of Levee District Police Special Response Team, the Michigan State Police Emergency Support Team, the New York State Police Mobile Response Team, and so on. Regardless of their titles, all receive training in special weapons and tactics.

At the pinnacle of American law enforcement stands the federal government, whose agents enforce federal laws nationwide—and, in some special cases, outside of the country. The first federal SWAT teams were FBI units, but other agencies soon followed the bureau's example. Today, active federal teams include the Bureau of Alcohol, Tobacco, Firearms, and Explosives Special Response Teams; the DEA's Mobile Enforcement Team and Foreign-deployed Advisory Support Teams; the State Department's Office of Mobile Security Deployments; the Department of Energy's Special Response Force; the U.S. Marshals Service's Special Operations Group; the Border Patrol's Patrol Tactical Unit; the Secret Service Counter Assault Team; plus Special Response Teams maintained by Immigration and Customs Enforcement, the Department of Energy, the U.S. Mint Police, and the U.S. Park Police.

Finally, various private corporations also train and operate SWAT teams, either to safeguard their own property or as contract security agents. In 2007 more than one million private security officers were employed throughout the United States, compared to 700,000 sworn law enforcement officers drawing government paychecks.[16] Some have full police powers within their areas of jurisdiction—power plants, exclusive residential communities, etc.—and are equipped for response to crisis situations. The Wackenhut Corporation, for example, guards the Liberty Bell in Philadelphia and screens all visitors to the Statue of Liberty in New York Harbor. In Canada, private SWAT teams such as the Durham Regional Nuclear Response Team and units employed by Bruce Power guard nuclear reactors.

WASHINGTON HELPS OUT

Special weapons, equipment, and training are expensive. Many of America's smaller law enforcement agencies could not afford SWAT teams until the 1980s, when federal assistance became available. The aid began in 1981, when Congress passed the Military Cooperation with Civilian Law Enforcement Agencies Act, and accelerated as Presidents Ronald Reagan and George H.W. Bush declared a series of so-called wars against crime and drugs. In September 1988, Congress passed a military appropriations bill that included $40 million for antidrug campaigns by the National Guard and Army Reserve.

LINNE GUNTHER

In 1959, when she was eight years old, Linne Gunther's father won a Nobel Prize for his work in nuclear physics. Thirty-three years later, Linne was a divorced mother of twin teenage sons. Deeply troubled by the state of world affairs and America's military actions, Gunther set off from her California home, driving across the country to stage a dramatic protest. At 11:00 A.M. on April 12, 1992, she drove a van onto the grounds of the United Nations headquarters in New York City, parking 30 yards from the organization's 38-story glass tower.

As guards approached the van, Gunther raised a can of gasoline, pouring the fuel over herself and the van's interior. The officers saw a box of kitchen matches tied around her neck. She also clutched a cigarette lighter and brandished contradictory signs. One read "This is a peaceful protest," while another warned that her van was "lined with explosives."[17]

Police were summoned, including a SWAT team, whose negotiators donned fireproof suits to approach the van. They distracted Gunther while other officers deflated the van's tires, immobilizing the vehicle. It hardly mattered, though, since Gunther had no plans to leave. Instead, she demanded TV time and a meeting with UN officials, to complain about tax money spent on foreign wars.

The standoff lasted 23 hours, until police arranged phone calls from two of Gunther's siblings, pleading for her surrender. At last, Gunther tossed two lighters out the window of her van and emerged on shaky legs to face arrest. She was booked on charges of attempted arson, reckless endangerment, and possession of an incendiary device. No explosives were found in the van.

While few (if any) military drug raids have occurred on U.S. soil, the Pentagon supplies civilian police with many weapons, vehicles, and other equipment commonly used in warfare. Between 1995 and

1997, Washington provided police with 5,985 assault rifles, 73 grenade launchers, and 112 armored personnel carriers. In 1997 alone, the outpouring of military gear exceeded 1.2 million items.[18]

That aid is also big business. In 1997 Congress created the Law Enforcement Support Program (LESP), based in Virginia, to streamline the transfer of military gear to police nationwide. Between January 1997 and October 1999 the LESP took 3.4 million orders from 11,000 police departments, spanning all 50 states. By December 2005, 17,000 agencies were doing business with the LESP, and while equipment was sold at discounted prices—as little as $1,000 for an armored vehicle normally costing $41,000—sales for 2005 still topped $727 million. The items purchased include 253 aircraft, 7,856 M16 assault rifles, 181 grenade launchers, 8,131 helmets, and 1,161 pairs of night-vision goggles.[19]

LAPD SWAT

Los Angeles, California

At 9:00 P.M. on February 6, 2008, Los Angeles police received a phone call from 20-year-old Edmund Rivera, announcing that he had just killed his father and two older brothers at the family home in suburban Winnetka. Some 200 officers, including members of LAPD's famous SWAT team, rushed to the house on Welby Way, where they found Rivera waiting, armed with a shotgun and pistol. A standoff ensued, with SWAT negotiators talking to Rivera by phone. He told them other people were alive inside the house, but refused to surrender. "Come get me," he said.[1]

At 12:30 A.M., SWAT accepted the challenge. Officers entered Rivera's home and found him waiting with his weapons. They exchanged fire, and Officers Randal Simmons and James Veenstra were hit, despite the body armor they were wearing. The rest of the team retreated under fire, hauling the wounded officers to safety, but it was too late for Simmons, who died at 1:00 A.M.

The siege dragged on. At 5:00 A.M. on February 7, officers lobbed tear-gas canisters into the house and rushed the door with a battering ram, but the door would not yield. Moments later, Rivera's stepmother escaped from the house, but Rivera himself stayed inside. By 7:30 the house was on fire, perhaps ignited by the gas grenades. Flames accomplished what tear gas and bullets could not, driving Rivera from his home with gun in hand. A SWAT sniper fired one shot, striking Rivera in the head and killing him instantly.

Inside the house, after firefighters extinguished the flames, police found the bodies of Rivera's father and two of his brothers. A fourth brother, who had his own apartment, was the family's lone survivor. LAPD spokesmen initially named Officer Simmons as the first SWAT member killed on duty, then recalled that Officer Louis Villalobos had died in 2000 during a SWAT training exercise. Officer Simmons remains the first SWAT member killed by a criminal during a team call-out.[2]

BIRTH OF A LEGEND

Modern mythology surrounds the LAPD SWAT team. Claims that it was the first such team are incorrect, although LAPD's unit was first to use the famous "SWAT" initials. Officer John Nelson proposed creation of the special team in 1967, and Inspector Darryl Gates (later LAPD's chief from 1978 to 1992) agreed. Gates planned to call the group a Special Weapons Assault Team, but his superiors changed it to Special Weapons and Tactics to give the unit a less aggressive image. The original unit had 15 four-man teams consisting of volunteers with military backgrounds. The teams conducted special training exercises once a month.[3]

SWAT's first major deployment in Los Angeles involved the Black Panther Party, a militant African-American group that mounted armed patrols in ghettos nationwide with the expressed intent of stopping racist police brutality. The Panthers angered police of all races by calling them "pigs," and the group engaged in shootouts with authorities from coast to coast during the late 1960s. Some of these incidents were provoked by police or FBI informants who had infiltrated the party, while others seemed to be unprovoked attacks on law enforcement.

There were several police–Panther shootings in Los Angeles in 1968–69. SWAT's confrontation with the party occurred on December 9, 1969, when the team raided Panther headquarters in search of two fugitives from justice. A four-hour siege left two officers and four Panthers wounded before 13 militants eventually surrendered. Nine suspects faced trial on multiple felony charges in July 1971, but testimony from Louis Tackwood—an informant for LAPD's Criminal Conspiracy Division—

persuaded jurors to dismiss the most serious charges; the Panthers were only convicted of conspiracy to possess illegal weapons. Even that charge seemed shaky, since the weapons in question—hand grenades—were purchased from a civilian coach of LAPD's SWAT team.[4]

Television star and producer Jack Webb gave SWAT its first national media exposure in January 1970, on an episode of *Adam-12,* a spin-off of Webb's long-running *Dragnet* series. That episode, like all of Webb's productions, featured a flattering depiction of the LAPD. When challenged by a friend who noted that his police dramas bore little resemblance to real life, Webb replied, "You know that, and now I know that. But that little old lady in Kansas will never know the difference."[5]

In 1971 LAPD's scattered SWAT teams were gathered into a single unit, designated as "D" Platoon of the department's Metropolitan Division. Its motto: "Uncompromised Duty, Honor and Valor."[6] Despite frequent call-outs, three more years elapsed before the team made national headlines again, in a pitched battle with the Symbionese Liberation Army (SLA).

"DEATH TO THE FASCIST INSECT"

The SLA was founded by convicted robber Donald DeFreeze soon after his escape from a California prison in March 1973. Calling himself "Field Marshal Cinque"—the name of an African tribesman who led a revolt aboard the slave ship *Amistad* in 1839—DeFreeze recruited a clique of radicals committed to overthrowing America's government. The SLA's name derived from symbiosis, a term describing cooperation between members of different species. (DeFreeze was the SLA's only African-American member; his followers were white, although some wore Afro wigs and blackface makeup as a rejection of their race.) In August 1973 the SLA declared war on the United States, vowing "Death to the fascist insect that preys upon the life of the people."[7] Violence soon followed.

In November 1973 two SLA members murdered Oakland's black superintendent of schools. Three months later, in nearby Berkeley, others kidnapped newspaper heiress Patricia Hearst and, according to her later testimony, brainwashed her into serving their cause. Hearst was present and armed with a rifle when SLA members robbed a San Francisco bank and wounded two customers in April 1974.

A Los Angeles Police Department (LAPD) officer holds a shotgun as he peers around a house toward the burning house where members of the Symbionese Liberation Army (SLA), the group responsible for kidnapping newspaper heiress Patricia Hearst, were holed up. Donald DeFreeze, leader of the SLA, and five followers died in the flames after a heated gunfight with LAPD officers and FBI SWAT teams. (*Bettmann/Corbis*)

After that incident, the "army" fled to L.A., where they occupied a house in the Compton ghetto. On May 16, 1974, two members tried to rob a local store, then fled and abandoned their car near the scene. A parking ticket in the glove compartment led police to their hideout on May 17, where LAPD and FBI SWAT teams engaged in a furious battle with the fugitives. The house caught fire at 6:41 P.M., but gunfire from inside continued until 7:01, when the structure collapsed. DeFreeze and five followers died in the wreckage—two shot by police, the others slain by fire and smoke-inhalation. Afterward, officers found 19 guns and 4,247 rounds of ammunition in the burned-out house. Although 668 of those cartridges were fired at authorities, no police were injured.[8]

HEROES SAVING LIVES

On June 3, 2006, Officers Joseph Meyer and Kristina Ripatti patrolled Los Angeles's Southwest Division, one of the city's most violent districts. As they cruised along a residential street, not far from the local police station, 52-year-old James McNeal ran in front of their car. The officers did not recognize McNeal, a career criminal, nor did they know that he was fleeing from the robbery of a neighborhood service station.

From the street, McNeal ran to his nearby home as Meyer and Ripatti pursued him on foot. On his porch, McNeal turned and drew a .22-caliber pistol, shooting Officer Ripatti twice at point-blank range. Her ballistic vest stopped one slug, but the other penetrated her chest through a gap beneath her left arm. Officer Meyer shot McNeal on the spot, killing him instantly, then radioed the alarm that police dread most: "Shots fired! Officer down!"[9]

Sergeant Robin Brown was first to arrive on the scene in response to that call, but she and Meyer were unable to stop the bleeding from Officer Ripatti's chest wound. Luckily, four SWAT team members—Officers Keith Bertonneau, Gary Koba, Gil Pinel, and Ralph Ward—were completing a neighborhood crime-suppression exercise nearby. All four were qualified emergency medical technicians via their SWAT training, and they reached the scene within one minute of Meyer's distress call, keeping Officer Ripatti alive until L.A. Fire Department paramedics Gerardo Puga and Adrian Vasquez arrived to transport her in their ambulance. Surgeons at California Hospital completed the process of saving Officer Ripatti's life, though her wound left her partially paralyzed from spinal damage.

Chief William Bratton subsequently awarded LAPD's Medal for Heroism to all concerned in the incident, including Officers Meyer, Ripatti, Bertonneau, Koba, Pinel, Ward, and Sergeant Brown, while the department's Golden Badge Foundation bestowed its own Exemplary Performance Award upon each

(continues)

(continued)

officer. Referring to the four SWAT officers, Chief Bratton said, "If it weren't for the immediate actions and professional training of these men, we would have lost Kristina that night. Not only did they save the life of a fellow police officer, they saved the life of a mother, daughter and wife."[10]

The producers of ABC television's *Extreme Makeover: Home Edition* noted Officer Ripatti's case and presented her family with a new house in December 2006. The house included an overhead track that can carry Ripatti through its rooms in response to voice commands. Despite her confinement to a wheelchair, Officer Ripatti gave birth to her second child, a son, in February 2008.

GOING HOLLYWOOD

Seven months after the SLA shootout, in February 1975, the television series *S.W.A.T.* premiered, with the first of 39 episodes depicting LAPD's team in action. Crime drama gave way to comedy in 1978 with the Pink Panther cartoon *Pink S.W.A.T.*, but firepower reigned supreme in 2003 as the former TV series was remade as a feature film starring Colin Farrell and Samuel L. Jackson. In that version, SWAT members fired for misconduct are paid to rescue a foreign drug lord from custody, foiled only when the true SWAT team steps in.[11]

The *real* Hollywood action, however, occurred on February 28, 1997, when crime partners Emil Matasareanu and Larry Phillips Jr. invaded a Bank of America branch in North Hollywood, armed with automatic rifles and dressed in homemade head-to-toe body armor. A passing police car saw them enter the bank and radioed for backup. Inside the bank, Matasareanu and Phillips fired 100 shots to terrify their 30 hostages, then bagged $305,305 from the bank's vault. They were leaving the bank at 9:38 A.M. when SWAT officers and TV news helicopters arrived on the scene.[12]

The ensuing battle was televised live across America and around the world. The bandits fired 1,300 shots, wounding several officers and civilian bystanders, while SWAT snipers tried to penetrate their armor. Patrol officers, outgunned, borrowed rifles from a nearby gunshop and rushed back to the firing line. Altogether, police fired at least 650 shots, inflicting 29 wounds on Matasareanu and 11 on Phillips. Larry Phillips ended the battle by shooting himself in the head. Matasareanu lay in the street for 40 minutes before dying.[13]

Matasareanu's relatives later sued LAPD, charging that officers denied him medical aid and thus let him bleed to death. Police spokesmen countered that ambulance attendants had refused to enter the "hot zone" until the bank and surrounding buildings were checked for possible gunmen at large. At trial in March 2000, federal jurors failed to reach a verdict on the lawsuit. Matasareanu's family dropped the case before a new trial was scheduled.[14]

THE ARMS RACE

The North Hollywood shootout changed the LAPD's thinking about on-duty weapons. All officers carried .38-caliber six-shot revolvers until 1987, when the department converted to 9mm Beretta semiautomatic pistols holding 15 rounds in their magazines. Each duty vehicle also contained a 12-gauge Ithaca Model 37 pump-action shotgun until the early 1990s, when corporate financial problems at Ithaca prompted a change to the Remington Model 870. Since 2002, new graduates of the LAPD police academy have been issued more powerful .40-caliber Glock semiautomatic pistols as their standard duty sidearm.

SWAT teams, predictably, use "special" weapons for their hazardous duty. Since 2002, SWAT's sidearm in Los Angeles is the .45-caliber Kimber Custom TLE (for *Tactical Law Enforcement*) II, renamed the Kimber LAPD SWAT Custom II TLE. The pistol holds 10 rounds and has a built-in firing pin safety which prevents accidental firing if the gun is dropped. Its tritium bar-dot sights are designed for accurate firing in darkness.

SWAT members carry the same 12-gauge shotguns issued to LAPD patrol officers, but some also use the Benelli M1 Super 90 Entry model, a shotgun that holds seven rounds of widely varied ammunition. Aside

FEMINIZING SWAT?

Inclusion in LAPD's SWAT team was reserved for men from 1967 until early 2008, when Chief William Bratton named Officer Jennifer Grasso as one of 13 new applicants cleared for special pre-admission training, scheduled to begin on March 31. At age 36, Officer Grasso was a veteran of LAPD's Metro Division held in high esteem by her colleagues. As one anonymous male member of the SWAT team told the *Los Angeles Times,* "Physically, she's a dynamo, and tactically she's very solid. She'd be a good selection." Grasso's supervisor, Sergeant Andrea Balter, confirmed that judgment. "I can't sing her praises nearly enough," Balter said.[15]

Officer Grasso would have joined the SWAT team in 2007, but she and several other applicants suffered injuries during their final screening tests on a U.S. Marine Corps obstacle course at Camp Pendleton, near San Diego. As a result of those injuries, Chief Bratton eliminated the Marine Corps test, saying that its challenges were "over-emphasizing physical prowess and tactical acumen."[16]

Officer Grasso was not the first woman to apply for SWAT duty. Officer Nina Acosta sued the LAPD in 1994, blaming sexual discrimination for the department's rejection of her SWAT application. She then changed her mind and resigned from the force when department leaders agreed to place her on the team.[17] That case, coupled with elimination of the old screening test, caused some critics to question whether any woman truly qualified for SWAT duty.

Early protests came from the Police Protective League (PPL), a union with 9,300 members, which accused the LAPD of "unfair labor practices" for changing SWAT admission standards without consulting the union. Challenged by Chief Bratton to prove any wrongdoing, PPL President Tim Sands told the *Times* that he considered Grasso "very highly qualified and I wish her the best of luck."[18]

Still, protests continued. In the *Los Angeles Daily News,* columnist Robert Parry claimed that during training Officer

Grasso "accidentally fired an MP5 submachine gun, without even having the weapon in a firing position." True or not, even Parry had to admit "that Jennifer Grasso is an outstanding cop. Those who have worked with her say she's far better than most male officers. SWAT officers I know were disappointed when she failed their stringent 2006 selection."[19]

Perhaps surprisingly, the harshest criticism of Chief Bratton's choice came from other women. One wrote, on the "LAPD Wife" Web site:

> Give me a break. What are we doing here, trying to create some GI Janes? There's no way a woman, no matter how smart or how fast she can run, can handle the job of SWAT. She just doesn't have the upper body strength. It's only something you can understand if you know how much [gear] they carry. There's no way a woman can run with that gear and drag one of her officers out of a building ect. [*sic*] Please don't debate me unless you've actually worked in SWAT and have experienced it first hand. The lady officers can use their intelligence by moving up to Detective, Sgt, captain but PLEASE don't try to be a member of SWAT.[20]

Clearly, the author of that post herself had never served with SWAT, and other police wives *did* dispute that view. One wrote:

> I don't agree with this at all! I'm very capable of pulling a grown man with full gear on out of anywhere and throwing him over my shoulder. I also know many other female officers who are capable of this. I carry more than one belt in the martial arts and Kravmaga. I can do 2,000 sit-ups on a bar upside down and 1,050 push ups with one hand in 11 minutes and 43 second—13 minutes since I've had the babies. There are so many things to consider like stamina, reflexes verses upper body strength....I high five Jennifer and I know she'll give it 110%.[21]

from standard buckshot loads and solid deer slugs capable of blasting through brick walls, this semiautomatic weapon may fire breaching rounds designed to smash door locks and hinges, which disintegrate on impact without wounding anyone inside the target room. Also available are flexible baton (or "beanbag") rounds, which are designed to stun a target without inflicting major injuries.

More specialized weapons favored by LAPD's SWAT team—and other teams nationwide—include the 9mm Heckler & Koch MP5 submachine gun in various forms, the same M16A2 assault rifle carried by U.S. military troops in combat, and the M4 carbine—a smaller, lighter version of the M16A2. Both rifles are chambered for .223-caliber (5.56x45mm NATO) ammunition and have an effective range of 600 yards. For precision shooting at longer ranges, SWAT snipers—or "designated marksmen"—rely on a variety of specialized high-powered rifles.

Even with such tools available, in the face of armed and hostile subjects, shooting is still the last resort. Success on a call-out is judged by *how few* deaths or injuries result (zero being the ideal).

UNDER SCRUTINY

Incidents like the North Hollywood shootout always provoke controversy. Another case that sparked heated criticism of the LAPD was the July 2005 SWAT shooting of Jose Peña and his infant daughter. In response to criticism of that action, Chief William Bratton convened a nine-member board of inquiry to investigate SWAT's use of force. Board members included famous attorneys Richard Aborn, William Geller, Gregory Longworth, and Eugene Ramirez; Merrick Bobb, the founding director of the Police Assessment Resource Center; Lieutenant Phil Hansen, commander of the L.A. County Sheriff's SWAT team; Chief Bernard Melekian of the Pasadena (California) Police Department; LAPD Officer Sharon Papa, formerly chief of the L.A. Metropolitan Transportation Authority during 1990–97; and Assistant Chief Linda Pierce, commander of the Seattle Police Department's Homeland Security Bureau.[22]

The board published its report on April 15, 2008, noting that LAPD's SWAT team had been called out 3,371 times between 1972 and 2005. The panel analyzed 696 shooting incidents occurring between the mid-1980s and 2005, concluding that 679 satisfied LAPD department guidelines, while two involved accidental gunfire and 15 cases had not been reviewed. Despite those generally positive findings—and attorney Aborn's description of SWAT as "the bravest of the brave"—the report charged that SWAT had become "insular, self-justifying and resistant to change." Furthermore, the panel found that "SWAT appeared at times to accelerate a tactical intervention or to have exacerbated the volatility of persons in an overly excited state, rather than negotiating or wait-ing for them to calm down or come off the effects of alcohol or drugs." Finally, the report stated, "Many board members were struck by these statistics and believed that it stretches credulity past the breaking point that no member of SWAT has ever engaged in an out-of-policy use of force, save for the two accidental discharges."[23]

Based on those findings, Chief Bratton ordered all SWAT officers to receive critical incident training geared toward coping with subjects who are mentally ill or "in an overly excited state." Forty percent of the unit's members had already received that training by 2008. The rest were expected to finish the course by mid-2009.[24]

Federal SWAT Teams

Fort A.P. Hill, Virginia

Gregory Rahoi was an outstanding FBI agent. A Wisconsin native, born in 1968, he joined the bureau at age 29, after serving as a police officer in Shorewood and Madison in Wisconsin. Prior to entering law enforcement, Rahoi was a paramedic and volunteer firefighter in Brookfield, Wisconsin; he then graduated with honors from Milwaukee's Marquette University in 1989 and earned a law degree from Marquette Law School four years later. Longtime friend and fellow Brookfield fireman Kenny Asselin nicknamed Rahoi "Mr. Public Safety." As Asselin told the *Milwaukee Journal Sentinel,* "Stuff always seemed to find Greg. If there was action that could be found, Greg didn't find it, it found him."[1]

Throughout his early career, Rahoi nurtured childhood dreams of joining the FBI. Natalie Rahoi told reporters that her son "had talked about wanting to go to the FBI all through high school," and that he was "elated" when the bureau accepted his application. Ken Asselin said, "There were no obstacles for Greg. When the guy had his mind set on something, he would accomplish it, whether [it was] going to law school or joining the FBI."[2] After training at the FBI Academy, Rahoi spent three years at the bureau's Chicago field office, then transferred to headquarters in Washington, D.C., where he joined the elite Hostage Rescue Team (HRT). His duties with that team included service in Afghanistan and Iraq, pursuing terrorists and guarding American diplomats.

December 2006 found Agent Rahoi back in the United States, joining in an HRT training exercise at Fort A.P. Hill, a U.S. Army base 60 miles south of Washington, D.C., near Bowling Green, Virginia. He had participated in many such sessions during his six years with the HRT, but this time something went horribly wrong. During a "live fire" exercise—when agents use deadly live ammunition instead of blanks— Agent Rahoi was shot and fatally wounded. He thus became the 50th FBI agent killed in the line of duty since 1925.[3]

Bureau spokesmen declined to comment on the circumstances of Rahoi's death, saying only that the case "is still under investigation." On December 11, 2006, during a memorial service at the FBI Academy in Quantico, Virginia, FBI Director Robert Mueller III awarded Rahoi the bureau's Medal of Valor for "brave and heroic acts occurring in the line of duty while deployed to Iraq as a member of the Hostage Rescue Team." No details were provided, but the medal is reserved for "exceptional acts of heroism or voluntary risk of personal safety and life."[4]

BIRTH OF A LEGEND

The FBI was created in 1908 and adopted its present, famous name in 1935, in the midst of a nationwide "crime war" that included deadly shootouts with bandits such as John Dillinger, "Baby Face" Nelson, and "Pretty Boy" Floyd. Five agents died in battle with gangsters during 1933–35,[5] but the bureau waited 40 years to create its first paramilitary units. During the early 1970s, inspired by the LAPD's example and alarmed by rising tides of terrorism, SWAT teams were organized within each of the FBI's 56 field offices. Fourteen larger, "enhanced" SWAT teams were also created nationwide, to assist local teams with extreme emergencies.[6] These measures, however, were not enough.

In 1982 U.S. Attorney General William Smith decided to create "a special counterterrorist unit within law enforcement to offer a tactical option for any extraordinary hostage crisis occurring within the United States." Thus was born the HRT, which formally began operations from the Washington, D.C., Metropolitan Field Office in 1983. Since then, according to HRT headquarters, the HRT has been called out on more than 200 occasions "in support of FBI terrorism, violent

An FBI Hostage Rescue Team is lowered from a helicopter during a practice demonstration at the FBI Training Academy in Quantico, Virginia. The exercise was meant to prepare team members for potential crisis situations at the 1984 Olympics in Los Angeles. (*Bettmann/Corbis*)

criminal, foreign counter-intelligence and other investigations. HRT has performed missions involving hostage rescue, barricaded subjects, high-risk arrest and warrant service (raids), and dive search. Additionally, the HRT has performed traditional law enforcement roles during hurricane relief operations, dignitary protection missions, tactical surveys, and on occasion, pre-positions in support of special events such as the Olympic Games, presidential inaugurations, and political conventions."[7]

THE SILENT BROTHERHOOD

One of the HRT's first adversaries was a group of homegrown neo-Nazi terrorists who called themselves The Order, or the *Brüder Schweigen*

("Silent Brotherhood," in German). Drawing inspiration from *The Turner Diaries,* a racist novel that also prompted Timothy McVeigh to carry out the deadly Oklahoma City bombing of April 19, 1995, members of The Order armed themselves for war against "ZOG"—the so-called Zionist Occupation Government in Washington, which they believed was run by Jewish communists bent on destroying the white "master race."

After some bungled counterfeiting schemes and small-time robberies, Order fanatics made their first headlines in June 1984, with the murder of Alan Berg, a controversial Jewish talk-radio host in Denver. Subsequently, they robbed several armored cars, including one California holdup that bagged $3.8 million. Leader Robert Jay Mathews shared the loot with various racist groups around the country and issued a formal declaration of war against ZOG.

Meanwhile, FBI agents pursued The Order with help from a member who faced federal counterfeiting charges, and through the serial number of a gun dropped during the California armored-car holdup. Mathews escaped one bureau ambush, but agents soon traced him to Whidbey Island, in Washington's Puget Sound. Cornered there by HRT members on December 8, 1984, Mathews chose to fight and died when FBI flares set fire to his cabin. Agents found him in the charred bathtub, with a gold medal of The Order melted into his chest.

Sweeping federal and state arrests followed, landing 29 of The Order's members in jail. Following guilty pleas and jury trials, 22 defendants received prison terms ranging from three years to 250 years. Six others received suspended sentences or credit for time served while awaiting trial.[8]

THE CSA

Another violent racist group, affiliated with The Order, was James Ellison's Covenant, Sword, and Arm of the Lord (CSA), based in northern Arkansas. CSA members manufactured illegal automatic weapons for other white-supremacist gangs, and carried out their own terrorist raids that included arson and bombings, armed robberies, at least two murders, and a bungled plot to assassinate a federal judge in Fort Smith, Arkansas.

Federal weapons violations brought the CSA under investigation by the Treasury Department's Bureau of Alcohol, Tobacco and Firearms (ATF), which obtained arrest warrants for various members in early 1985. Because the CSA's Arkansas compound was fortified and heavily armed, HRT agents joined the ATF to serve those warrants on April 20, 1985. The agents came ready for battle, but after a four-day siege, Ellison and his followers surrendered peacefully. Facing 20 years in prison if convicted on all charges, Ellison agreed to testify against other racist leaders in return for leniency. He was a key prosecution witness in April 1988 at the trial of 13 neo-Nazi activists on charges of sedition

MIAMI SHOOTOUT (1986)

As the LAPD's SWAT team learned hard lessons from the North Hollywood shootout, so FBI headquarters studied a gruesome case from April 1986. Miami agents had spent 18 months tracking a pair of unknown subjects linked to several violent bank robberies and the murder of a man whose car was stolen for a local holdup when an alarm sent them racing to another bank on April 11. A high-speed chase began, with several carloads of FBI agents pursuing two men in a stolen Chevrolet Monte Carlo. The chase ended when the bandits drove down a dead-end street and crashed their car into a tree.

The feds still didn't know whom they were chasing. Inside the Monte Carlo sat William Matix and Michael Platt, two gun-loving U.S. Army veterans who had staged Miami's recent rash of holdups, shooting several people in the process. Later evidence suggested that Matix and Platt had formed a murder pact beforehand, after meeting in the service, and had killed each other's wives. Together, they ran a landscaping business created as a "front" to launder profits from their heists.

Agents outnumbered Platt and Matix four to one on April 11, but the gunmen came out blasting with a .223-caliber Ruger Mini-14 semiautomatic rifle, a 12-gauge shotgun, and

(conspiracy to overthrow a lawful government), but despite his testimony and that of several other confessed criminals, jurors acquitted all of the defendants.

In other courtrooms, nine CSA members pled guilty to manufacturing or selling illegal weapons, receiving prison terms that ranged from 18 months to five years. Cult member Richard Snell, convicted of murdering a pawn broker whom he mistakenly thought was Jewish, received a death sentence and was executed in April 1995, on the same day Timothy McVeigh bombed Oklahoma City's federal building.[9]

two .357 Magnum revolvers. The agents fought back with their handguns and one riot shotgun, suffering terrible losses in the process. When the gun smoke cleared, Agents Jerry Dove and Benjamin Grogan were dead, and five of their six companions were wounded. Agent Edmundo Mireles finally killed both bandits, despite a crippling wound to his left arm, but the pair seemed almost indestructible in battle. Between them, Matix and Platt were shot 18 times—and nearly escaped in an FBI car—before Agent Mireles finished them off at close range.[10]

A study of the Miami shootout concluded that pistols normally carried by FBI agents—either .38-caliber revolvers or 9mm semiautomatics—were not powerful enough for combat with well-armed felons. Despite hits scored by five different agents using six weapons, Platt and Matix fought on. Today, agents carry semiautomatic handguns chambered for the larger .40-caliber (10.2mm) Smith & Wesson cartridge, including various models such as Smith & Wesson's Model 4006 (which holds 11 rounds) and the Glock 22 (15 shots) or Glock 23 (13 rounds). FBI field offices and some duty vehicles are also now equipped with military-style assault rifles and submachine guns to counter the firepower of heavily armed criminals.

RUBY RIDGE

Yet another neo-Nazi caused trouble for the HRT in 1992. Randy Weaver, an associate of the racist Aryan Nations, built an isolated home for his family near that group's Idaho headquarters in the 1980s. In January 1985 the U.S. Secret Service investigated complaints that Weaver had stockpiled illegal weapons and threatened the president of the United States, but they filed no charges.

In October 1989 ATF agents accused Weaver of selling two illegal sawed-off shotguns to an informant in the Aryan Nations. Weaver denied it, claiming the agents bought legal shotguns and shortened the barrels themselves, to "frame" him. Eight months later, when Weaver refused to become an ATF informant, agents filed charges and arrested him. After posting bail, Weaver retreated to his cabin on Ruby Ridge and failed to appear for his scheduled trial in March 1991. Much later, court officials admitted telling Weaver the wrong trial date, but in the meantime, they issued a new arrest warrant.

The task of jailing Weaver fell to members of the U.S. Marshals Service, six of whom approached Weaver's rural home on August 21, 1992. Weaver's dogs pursued the marshals, followed by his 14-year-old son and houseguest Kevin Harris, both armed with rifles. Shots were fired, killing Deputy Marshal William Degan, Samuel Weaver, and one of the dogs. Harris fled (with a slug in his back) to the house, where Randy Weaver and his wife and two daughters prepared for a siege.

The U.S. Marshals called for FBI assistance, bringing HRT agents to Ruby Ridge. On August 22, HRT sniper Lon Horiuchi wounded Randy Weaver and killed his wife Vicki, but the standoff still dragged on until August 31, when the Weavers and Harris finally surrendered. In April 1993 Weaver and Harris faced trial for Deputy Marshal Deegan's murder and various lesser offenses. Jurors acquitted Kevin Harris on all counts, and convicted Randy Weaver only on the minor charge of failure to appear for trial in his firearms case. He received an 18-month sentence (with credit for 14 months served prior to trial) and a $10,000 fine.[11]

While those verdicts upset the federal government, worse lay in store. Investigators learned that Vicki Weaver was killed while holding a 10-month-old baby in her arms, a result of FBI "rules of engagement" that authorized use of deadly force without a demand for surrender. Justice Department spokesmen called that shooting "inexcusable," but took no action against Agent Horiuchi since he was following official orders when he fired the fatal shot. A two-year internal review of the siege produced letters of censure for five of Horiuchi's superiors; two of those received 15-day suspensions, and one was suspended for 10 days. The Weavers filed a wrongful-death lawsuit, then settled out of court: Randy Weaver received $100,000, while his daughters got $1 million each. Kevin Harris received a $380,000 settlement.[12]

CRITICAL INCIDENTS

While shaken by events at Ruby Ridge and the bloody Branch Davidian siege at Waco, Texas, in 1993, the HRT persevered, refined its methods, and renewed commitment to its motto: *Servare Vitas* ("To Save Lives," in Latin). One step in that direction was the formation of a new Critical

Members of one of several elite FBI Hostage Rescue Teams conduct their mission briefing before lifting off. (*AFP/Getty Images*)

MONTANA FREEMEN

Three years after the Branch Davidian tragedy in Texas, HRT agents faced another armed standoff with a band of anti-government extremists who called themselves the Montana Freemen. Their political philosophy denied any state or federal government authority, claiming that every individual is "sovereign," beholden to no higher law. In pursuit of that goal, the Freemen bought land near Jordan, Montana, and founded "Justus Township," complete with a private bank and "common-law court."

Freemen leader LeRoy Schweitzer and others filed nuisance lawsuits against local elected officials, charging official misconduct, then filed liens (claims on personal property) against the defendants and illegally sold the bogus liens to foreign buyers, announcing a plan to pay off America's national debt with the proceeds. No such payments were made, however, and the Freemen also balked at paying state and federal taxes. In March 1996 cult member Lavon Hanson stumbled into an FBI sting operation, telling undercover agents that he would transport illegally earned funds from Los Angeles to the

Incident Response Group (CIRG), created by FBI Director Louis Freeh to plan ahead for future siege and hostage situations, which would ideally be resolved without loss of life. The CIRG's four subdivisions include an Operations Support Branch, a Tactical Support Branch, a Technical Support Branch, and a Strategic Information and Operations Center based in Quantico, Virginia.[13]

HRT members are FBI agents first and foremost. Applications are accepted from agents 23 to 36 years old who possess at least three years of military combat training—preferably with elite units such as the Navy SEALs or Army Special Forces—and/or SWAT team experience. All applicants are screened through rigorous physical fitness tests, drug testing, detailed background investigation, polygraph (lie detector)

Freemen compound in Montana. Agents filed criminal charges, but arresting the Freemen posed problems.

Remembering Waco, and dreading another run-in with a possible suicide cult, HRT agents surrounded Justus Township for 81 days, between March 25 and June 13, 1996. Negotiations took the place of raids, tear gas, and gunfire, ending with a peaceful resolution to the siege and the arrest of 18 subjects. Four pled guilty, while the rest were convicted at a chaotic trial, marked by outbursts from the defendants and attempts to "arrest" the judge in court. Schweitzer received the longest prison term—22 years and six months—on charges that included conspiracy, armed robbery, firearms violations, bank fraud, mail and wire fraud, threatening public officials, interstate transportation of stolen property, and lying under oath to the Internal Revenue Service. Jail terms for the other defendants ranged from time served pending trial to 15 years. Defendant Russell Dean Landers received an initial sentence of 11 years and three months, but the sentence was extended for 15 more years in April 2008 when Landers was caught attempting to extort his release from custody with more bogus financial claims.[14]

examinations, and a series of interviews conducted by current HRT personnel. The HRT's "enhanced" physical fitness screening judges applicants on timed performance in a 300-meter sprint and a 1.5-mile run, plus a minimum number of push-ups, pull-ups, and sit-ups. Initial fitness tests are performed at the applicant's assigned FBI field office, with advance warning that actual HRT training "will require physical fitness well in excess of these minimums." Applicants have three chances to pass the fitness test during a six-month period, but triple failure permanently bars them from an HRT assignment.[15]

Agents who clear the early hurdles next begin a four-month training period in which they learn the fine points of HRT duties, including hostage rescue, apprehending barricaded subjects, mobile and airborne assaults, counter-terrorism, protection of dignitaries on U.S. soil or protection of FBI personnel overseas, and assistance with military special missions. Indeed, the training never ends, for even when assigned to active duty teams, HRT members rotate through endless 60-day cycles of training, operations, and support. The training cycle maintains vital skills and instructs HRT members in use of new weapons or other equipment. During an operations cycle, a team is available for call-outs on a moment's notice. The support cycle includes maintenance of HRT equipment, plus unspecified "special projects."

HRT AT SEA

While most critical incident scenarios involve action against armed subjects or terrorists on dry land, the Maritime Transportation Security Act of 2002 also requires the FBI and U.S. Coast Guard to cooperate in protection of American seaports—and, potentially, to intercede in hostage crises at sea. In a March 2006 report from the Inspector General's Office, FBI headquarters acknowledged that its 56 field-office SWAT teams were not adequately trained for maritime operations, but they placed full faith in the HRT. Some tension was revealed between the bureau and the Coast Guard's 13 Maritime Safety and Security Teams—especially in cases when the HRT needed Coast Guard vessels for transport to targets—but the agencies sought to resolve those differences through completion of a detailed Maritime Operational Threat Response (MOTR) plan.[16]

That plan also incorporates the FBI's Hazardous Devices Response Unit, formed in 2004 to handle threats involving toxic substances and weapons of mass destruction. As detailed in federal documents, the MOTR plan seeks to clarify Coast Guard and FBI duties in a maritime emergency, thus avoiding any conflicts or needless confusion. Leaders of both agencies sought assurances that they were not "competing for the same resources" or wasting time with duplicate efforts. The final MOTR plan, issued in October 2005 and subject to revisions as needed, created an interagency Maritime Security Working Group to resolve difficulties before an actual emergency occurs. Subsequent training exercises, with detailed "after-action reports," theoretically resolved outstanding issues.[17]

The Inspector General's report of March 2006 closed with recommendations that FBI Headquarters "ensure that all field offices submit critical incident reports to the CIRG by January 15 each year; require the FBI's Maritime Security Program, in consultation with the CIRG, to use the reports to conduct maritime-specific reviews of the FBI's crisis management policies and practices—including any requirements for field office crisis management plans—and to disseminate maritime-related lessons learned and best practices."[18]

Special Weapons and Tactics

Denver, Colorado

Racism and racially motivated violence are major components of United States history. It was remarkable, therefore, when members of the Democratic Party gathered to nominate Barack Obama—son of a black Kenyan native who met his white American wife in Hawaii—as their presidential candidate in August 2008. Obama had earned the nomination by winning a series of hotly contested primary elections, and his campaign had sparked threats from white racists dating back to May 2007.

It came as no surprise, then, that security was tight around Denver's Pepsi Center, where the Democratic National Convention was held during August 25–28. It was so tight, in fact, that Denver's civic leaders spent $18.2 million on new police equipment for convention week. Rumors spread that high-tech SWAT teams would be standing by with sonic (sound-wave) weapons and "goo guns," designed to immobilize violent protesters or terrorists. Those rumors, in turn, prompted a lawsuit by the American Civil Liberties Union to force disclosure of items obtained by Denver police before the convention.

While sonic weapons have been tested by military forces around the world in recent decades, and the U.S. Army once considered use of paralyzing goo guns before deeming them impractical, no such tools had been purchased in Denver. Still, Mayor John Hickenlooper balked at releasing specific details of what *was* acquired, and Denver Police Department Deputy Chief Michael Battista told the *Rocky Mountain News,* "I'm purchasing equipment that's going to protect my officers, and to try and defeat what they're trying to accomplish—the unlawful activity they're trying to accomplish. So if they know what tools I have, then they'll build their plan to defeat my tools."[1]

In the final event, no protesters were blasted with sound waves or glued to the sidewalk with fast-drying slime. Obama received the Democratic nomination, as expected, and went on to win election in November as America's first mixed-race president.

The racist threats continued. On October 24, 2008, ATF agents arrested two members of the "Supreme White Alliance" for stockpiling illegal weapons, threatening Obama's life, and plotting a multistate murder spree meant to claim the lives of 102 African Americans. The plotters allegedly hoped to shoot 88 victims—"88" is a common racist tattoo, standing for "HH" (eighth letter of the alphabet), or "Heil Hitler!"—and decapitate 14 more, in honor of a racist slogan dubbed the "14 Words," penned from prison by convicted Nazi killer David Lane.[2] Three months later, Secret Service agents jailed a white Mississippi resident for posting threats against Obama on racist Web sites.[3]

SPECIAL WEAPONS

Most American police officers carry firearms in addition to various nonlethal weapons, including various clubs, chemical sprays, or electric stun guns. What is it, then, that makes SWAT weapons unique?

For most cops in the United States and around the world, the basic weapon is a handgun or pistol, easily concealable and designed to be fired one-handed, with or without support from the free hand in aiming. Because Samuel Colt's revolvers were considered especially unlikely to jam compared to early semiautomatic pistols, most American law enforcement agencies insisted that their officers carry "wheelguns" on duty, often dictating specific calibers. During the last quarter of the 20th century, many departments switched to semiautomatic pistols, though some resisted, claiming that semiautomatic weapons were less accurate and jammed too often to be practical in combat. America's military challenged that claim by adopting the Colt .45-caliber automatic in 1911, then switching to the 15-shot Beretta Model 92 in 1985. By the year 2000, most police departments allowed or required their officers to carry semiautomatic handguns, including the popular Berettas and Glocks, in various calibers.

SWAT demands a little "something extra" from its pistols, in terms of both reliability and stopping power. Although most SWAT officers rely on other weapons first, holding their pistols in reserve, close-quarters battle (CQB) sometimes requires a backup weapon that will stop a violent adversary in his tracks. While LAPD's SWAT team chose the .45-caliber Kimber Custom TLE II, other teams place their trust in sidearms such as the SIG P226 (.40-caliber) or P229 (including a .357 Magnum model), the Glock 21 (.45-caliber) or 23 (.40-caliber), or the Heckler & Koch USP Tactical (available in 9mm, .40-caliber, .45-caliber). All have high-capacity magazines, more than double the load of a standard six-shot revolver, and their ammunition has been battle-tested for maximum stopping power.

Many American police cars come equipped with *shotguns,* smooth-bore weapons that normally fire clumps of pellets (or "shot") in various sizes—thus the nickname "scattergun"—but which may also use different kinds of specialized ammunition as required. Officers on routine patrol commonly carry pump-action shotguns chambered for 12-gauge ammunition. (In olden times, "gauge"—or "bore," in Europe—was calculated by the number of steel balls having the same diameter as a shotgun's barrel which make up one pound. Thus, the *smaller* the gauge, the *larger* the weapon's caliber.) No American police department presently issues semiautomatic shotguns as standard equipment, but those rapid-fire weapons are found in SWAT arsenals. Popular models include the Benelli M3 (featuring a switch to change from semiauto to pump-action as desired) and M1014 (strictly semiautomatic, adopted by the U.S. Marine Corps in 1999), the Franchi SPAS-12 (also alternating semiauto fire with pump-action) and SPAS 15 (with a detachable magazine resembling an assault rifle's), the Remington 1100 (semiauto version of the widely used pump-action 870 model), and the Mossberg 930 (Model 935 in camouflage colors).

While police and soldiers favor buckshot in battle—again, numbered by size, from No. 4 (.26-caliber) to 000 (.36-caliber)—other shotgun ammunition includes solid slugs pre-cut with rifling grooves for greater accuracy, various breaching rounds designed to shatter door locks or hinges without wounding a room's occupants, bolo rounds (two or more slugs, linked by steel wire), flechette rounds (loaded with steel darts), "nonlethal" baton rounds designed to stun humans, and rock salt intended to cause pain while dispersing crowds.

Next up the scale of SWAT weapons come submachine guns, lightweight weapons capable of fully automatic fire (continuous fire while the trigger is depressed) or selective fire (switching from full-auto to semiauto as the shooter requires). Originally, submachine guns were designed to fire pistol ammunition—and are thus called "machine pistols" in many foreign nations—while light or medium machine guns fired rifle cartridges and heavy machine guns used their own distinct ammunition. Today, the line between weapons is blurred by some companies—notably Colt and certain Eastern European manufacturers—whose "submachine guns" are simply smaller versions of their popular assault rifles, more properly called carbines. American SWAT teams favor German-made Heckler & Koch submachine guns, including variations of the H&K MP5 introduced in 1966, or the less-expensive H&K UMP (*Universale Maschinenpistole*, or "Universal Machine Pistol"). Both weapons are available in 9mm, 10mm, or .40-caliber Smith & Wesson, firing 650 to 800 shots per minute in full-auto mode.

All SWAT teams use rifles—weapons meant to be aimed and fired from the shoulder, with spiral grooves ("rifling") etched inside the barrel to spin bullets for greater range and accuracy—both for CQB action and long-distance sniping. Entry teams use military-style assault rifles, which are normally selective-fire weapons. Federal assistance programs have furnished police with thousands of M16 rifles (adopted by the U.S. military in 1964) and more recent variants including the M16A2 and M16A4, modified to eliminate problems that early M16s suffered during jungle combat in Vietnam. Some teams also use foreign-made rifles, such as the Heckler & Koch G3—a .30-caliber weapon (7.62mm) as opposed to the M16's .223-caliber (5.56mm). Worldwide, many police SWAT teams use the assault rifles issued to their nation's armed forces, including the globally popular Steyr AUG (*Armee Universal Gewehr*, or "Universal Army Rifle"), manufactured in Austria since 1978.

Military aid programs have also supplied many American SWAT teams with carbines, shortened rifles originally designed for use by mounted cavalry troops. Today, military and police carbines are shrunken versions of standard assault rifles, commonly including the parent weapon's selective-fire capability. Carbines derived from the M16 include Colt's CAR-15 and M4, featuring shortened barrels and collapsing stocks. Heckler & Koch also offers the G36, a shortened version of its G3 rifle, and the HK416, designed specifically to compete with the Colt M4 carbine.

"LESS-LETHAL" WEAPONS

Despite the image of SWAT promoted in fiction and film, use of deadly force is the worst-case scenario, withheld as a last resort in the most extreme situations. For that reason, SWAT also employs various nonlethal weapons, more properly labeled compliance weapons, and sometimes dubbed "less-lethal," since most can kill if used improperly or against certain targets.[4]

Compliance weapons, as their name suggests, are designed to make difficult subjects comply with police demands for surrender. Ideally, they compel violent subjects to drop any weapons and cease struggling without inflicting permanent injury. All theoretically stun or disorient targets in various ways, though any specific individual's reactions are unpredictable and can vary depending on size and strength, mental state, or ingestion of drugs.

Most police officers carry some kind of club, baton, or other manual weapon designed for striking during violent confrontations. All may produce fatal injuries if used improperly, and SWAT officers, although trained in hand-to-hand combat techniques, are generally not expected to grapple bare-handed with subjects. Instead, they often rely on special firearms ammunition developed to cause numbing pain or unconsciousness without killing the human target.

The first less-lethal police ammunition consisted of rock-salt shotgun shells used to sting and disperse rioters. Lead pellets of bird shot

BODY ARMOR

SWAT team members wear various forms of protective gear on call-outs. Some are as simple as plastic goggles (20 percent of all SWAT injuries involve the eyes[5]) and knee and elbow pads. All SWAT members wear some kind of body armor, which has saved the lives of some 3,000 American police officers since the mid-1970s.[6]

No armor is truly bulletproof—and some that stop high-caliber bullets will not deflect knives—but any form of protection is useful in combat. The National Institute of Justice ranks body armor in six classes, according to the firearms ammunition it deflects.[7] Those classes include the following:

* *Type I*: protects against .22-caliber bullets up to 2.6 grams in weight, striking at speeds of 1,050 feet per second (fps) or less, and against .380-caliber bullets up to 6.2 grams, traveling 1,025 fps or less
* *Type II-A*: deflects 9mm bullets of eight grams or less, traveling 1,090 fps or less, and .40-caliber S&W bullets of 11.7 grams or less, at 1,025 fps or slower
* *Type II*: guards against 9mm rounds of eight grams, impacting at 1,175 fps or less, and .357 Magnum rounds up to 10.2 grams, traveling 1,400 fps or less
* *Type III-A*: safe against 9mm rounds up to eight grams and 1,400 fps, and .44 Magnum bullets up to 15.6 grams and speeds of 1,400 fps or less
* *Type III*: safe against .30-caliber rifle bullets of 9.6 grams, striking at 2,750 fps, and all bullets covered by lower classes of armor
* *Type IV*: offers the highest level of protection, including deflection of .30-caliber armor-piercing rifle bullets up to 10.8 grams, traveling at 2,850 fps; often includes ceramic materials designed for greater resistance to impacts

were used for the same purpose until a 1969 incident in Berkeley, California, left one antiwar protester blind and another with pellets embedded in his heart.[8] Modern less-lethal projectiles include baton rounds made from rubber, plastic, wax, or wood, and flexible baton rounds, also known as "bean-bag" rounds. While designed to stun without killing, baton rounds may cause fatal injuries. In Northern Ireland between 1973 and 1981, police fired more than 42,000 baton rounds at protest marchers and rioters, killing 14 persons (including nine children) with shots to the chest that caused heart failure.[9]

Less-lethal stunning force may also be delivered by concussion grenades, nicknamed "flash-bangs." Unlike grenades designed to kill or wound with sharp fragments, concussion grenades have casings made of thin, soft metal or tar-coated cardboard. Flash-bangs may stun their targets with sound alone (the *bang*), or with a combination of sound and blinding light (the *flash*). Some also contain hard-rubber balls that fly around a room when the grenade detonates, serving the same function as baton rounds fired from guns. Concussion grenades rarely cause permanent injury, but a subject's eardrums may be damaged, and falling may result in broken bones, internal injuries, or death.

Electroshock weapons have been used by American police since the 1960s, when various Southern departments used shock-prods against civil rights protesters. Created for use with livestock—hence the popular "cattle prod" label—shock-prods scandalized the South when used against children and peaceful demonstrators. Some were also used as torture devices in Southern jails and prisons, increasing protests against racist law enforcement below the Mason-Dixon Line. Modern electroshock weapons—collectively known as stun-guns or Tasers (though that name properly applies only to weapons manufactured since 1993 by Taser International, in Scottsdale, Arizona)—are more powerful than old-style prods and are designed specifically for incapacitating humans.

Stun-guns use electric current to disrupt the body's motor functions, resulting in muscle spasms and temporary paralysis. Basic models operate by manually pressing the weapon's electrodes against a subject's body and triggering the charge. These weapons come in many forms, including some that resemble pistols and others disguised within flashlights. For subduing violent subjects at a distance, some stun-guns fire darts attached to wires, like small harpoons, that penetrate the target's flesh and transmit voltage from the launcher in an officer's hand. Taser International has also announced production of XREP (an eXtended *Range Electro-Muscular Projectile*), which contains its own battery and may be fired up to 100 yards from a 12-gauge shotgun. Less successful delivery methods, tried and rated as failures in Europe, include electrified water cannons and the "Plasma Taser" developed by Germany's Rheinmetall firm in 2003, using an electrified gas in aerosol form. The Plasma Taser's 10-foot maximum range, combined with unintended "gassing" of bystanders, made the weapon impractical.

Finally, *chemical weapons* are used by police in various forms to subdue combative subjects. *Lachrymatory agents* irritate the eyes, producing tears and causing temporary blindness, while other chemicals attack the nose and throat, briefly simulating suffocation. Common "tear gas" (xylyl bromide) evolved during World War I (1914–18) for military use and was employed thereafter by police worldwide against rioters and barricaded subjects, delivered in the form of grenades or canisters fired from guns. During the 1950s and 1960s, British labs produced two new forms of debilitating gas—CR (dibenzoxazepine) and CS (a powdered form of 2-chlorobenzalmalononitrile)—which have largely replaced xylyl bromide. Both still have drawbacks, including limited effects on some humans and unpredictable wind-borne dispersal when discharged in open spaces.

Lake Erie Chemical Corporation, formerly a branch of Smith & Wesson, pioneered aerosol chemical spray in 1962 with the development of "Chemical Mace." Mace combined the chemicals 2-butanol, propylene glycol, cyclohexene, and dipropylene glycol methyl ether as lachrymatory agents, delivered at short range from handheld dispensers. More recently, many police have switched to "pepper spray," also called "OC spray" after its primary irritant, oleoresin capsicum, which is derived from the capsicum pepper plant. Aside from aerosol sprays, pepper gas has also been delivered since the 1990s in "pepperball" projectiles, adapted from paintball ammunition and filled with liquid or powdered oleoresin capsicum.

As with other less-lethal weapons, problems may arise from the use of pepper spray. In 1995 the American Civil Liberties Union documented

26 deaths from police applications of OC, equivalent to one death for every 600 recorded uses of pepper spray nationwide.[10] Two years before that report was published, the U.S. Army completed tests on pepper spray at Maryland's Aberdeen Proving Grounds, announcing that OC could produce "mutagenic effects [DNA mutations], carcinogenic effects [cancer], sensitization, cardiovascular and pulmonary toxicity, neurotoxicity, as well as possible human fatalities. There is a risk in using this product on a large and varied population."[11]

SPECIAL TACTICS

SWAT operations, with or without the violence of close-quarters battle, require special training and preparation. While normal training

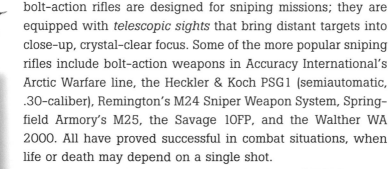

SNIPERS

SWAT snipers are the team's long-range marksmen, armed with rifles designed for pinpoint accuracy. They often work with *observers* who help calculate distance and protect the sniper from surprise attacks while he is focused on a target. Various mechanical *range finders* assist those calculations and determine whether wind or other factors may affect a shot. When given the "green light," snipers may provide *diversionary fire* as a distraction or use deadly force to achieve a standoff's solution.[12]

Since accuracy is paramount for snipers, they do not use automatic weapons. Many different semiautomatic or manual bolt-action rifles are designed for sniping missions; they are equipped with *telescopic sights* that bring distant targets into close-up, crystal-clear focus. Some of the more popular sniping rifles include bolt-action weapons in Accuracy International's Arctic Warfare line, the Heckler & Koch PSG1 (semiautomatic, .30-caliber), Remington's M24 Sniper Weapon System, Springfield Armory's M25, the Savage 10FP, and the Walther WA 2000. All have proved successful in combat situations, when life or death may depend on a single shot.

theoretically prepares SWAT officers for any possible emergency—including practice shooting from "wounded" positions in case they suffer injuries—they are not psychics and cannot predict where they will be called out to lead a high-risk raid or lay siege to a barricaded subject.

Once a call-out has occurred, the first step toward resolution is detailed planning. All possible information about the target must be obtained, including floor plans, electrical wiring diagrams, any hidden entrances, and so on. Officers must also determine how many persons are inside a target building or vehicle, including both suspects and hostages. Unidentified stray individuals pose a life-threatening risk to all concerned.

Whenever possible, SWAT officers enhance their knowledge of a target by surveillance, using any high-tech tools available. These tools include cameras, listening devices (or "bugs"), radar, and thermal-imaging equipment that detects body heat.

Inside views of the target may be obtained using pinhole cameras (inserted through small holes drilled in walls, floors, or ceilings) and fiber-optical cameras attached to thin wires that may also be inserted through cracks around doors or windows, along heating or air-conditioning vents, and so forth. Wide-angle ("fish-eye") lenses provide a broad visual field and may cover 360 degrees if the camera can be rotated.

SWAT can eavesdrop on conversations and other sounds inside a target building with various kinds of microphones, either placed inside the building or operated from a distance. Spike-mikes, like pinhole cameras, are inserted from holes drilled by officers outside the room or building. Fiber-optical microphones, likewise, operate in the same way as fiber-optical cameras. Directional microphones—sometimes called "shotgun microphones"—are aimed from a distance but function best in open spaces and may not capture sounds through intervening walls. Laser microphones direct a beam of light at glass windowpanes or other surfaces that transmit sound waves, capture the material's vibrations, and convert it back into audible sound through a remote receiver.

When every available tool has been used, and if negotiations with a barricaded subject fail, SWAT officers must conduct an entry. Entries may be stealth (slow and secret) or dynamic (swift and aggressive), but in either case, surprise is critical. Subjects alerted in advance are far more dangerous than those caught unaware.

Stealth entry may involve opening doors, windows, or skylights, and crawling through air ducts or climbing down elevator shafts—any maneuver, in short, that takes the subject by surprise.

Dynamic entry is more likely to result in violence, and calls for special skills.

First, every member of a SWAT team must know his or her area of responsibility (AOR). Snipers and observers watch the action from a distance, covering their team, and may help with diversionary fire to distract the subjects. Other members of the team form a single-file procession called a "snake," arranged in accordance to their duties. They include

- a point man (or woman), who leads the team as officers leave their last cover and concealment (LCC) to approach the target, dealing with any immediate danger along the way[13]

A SWAT sniper *(right)* and an observer participate in a training exercise on a sniper course with a moving target. During a siege, snipers and observers view the mission from a distance, providing cover and valuable information for their team. (*AP Photo/*Palo Alto Daily News*, Tony Avelar)*

Members of the Passaic County (New Jersey) Sheriff's Department SWAT Team ride on the outside of their new BearCat armored vehicle during a day of training exercises. (*AP Photo/Joe Epstein, The Record of Bergen County*)

- one or more kickers, assigned to breach doors with tools that include battering rams, pry bars, and customized explosive charges [14]
- a cover-man or post-man, first to penetrate the target and secure the entrance against any threats [15]
- a pickup man or cleanup man, often the team's leader, trusted to make sure that nothing is forgotten, either in terms of equipment or planning [16]
- a medic, trained to provide first-aid to any officers, hostages, or subjects injured during the action. As with all other team members, the medic is also fully trained in all aspects of CQB [17]
- a rear guard or tail gunner, placed at the rear of the "snake" to prevent any nasty surprises from hidden gunmen or anyone else who may approach the team from its rear without warning or authorization [18]

In many situations, armored vehicles provide cover for an advancing SWAT team. These come in many shapes and sizes and are produced by various manufacturers; they may include the team's basic van, truck, or other transport vehicle. Lenco Armored Vehicles, established in 1981, bills itself as America's "leading designer and manufacturer of tactical armored security vehicles,"[19] but it has many competitors, including Alpine Armoring, AM General, Custom Armored Vehicles, Texas Armoring Corporation, Transeo Global Vehicle Solutions, and Britain's Alvis Saracen. The cost of armored vehicles prevents some police departments from using them, but many military-surplus models have been purchased at discount rates from the federal government.

Hostage Negotiation

London, England

At 11:30 A.M. on April 30, 1980, six terrorists invaded the Iranian embassy located at No. 16 Princess Gate in London, firing shots into the walls and capturing 26 hostages. The gunmen identified themselves as members of the Democratic Revolutionary Movement for the Liberation of Arabistan—their name for Khūzestān Province in southwestern Iran. Their message to the media was brief: "One: We demand our human and legitimate rights. Two: We demand freedom, autonomy and recognition of the Arabistan people. Three: We demand the release of 91 Arab prisoners in Arabistan. If all the demands are not met by noon on Thursday, May 1, the Embassy and all the hostages will be blown up."[1]

Unknown to the invaders, a constable assigned to guard the embassy triggered a silent alarm that brought members of the Metropolitan Police Department's Antiterrorist Squad rushing to Princess Gate. They alerted the Special Air Service (SAS) in Hereford, mobilizing that elite group's Counter Revolutionary Warfare Wing. SAS members examined the embassy grounds and prepared an assault plan using a scale model of the five-story target.

That night, the terrorists reported that two of their captives were ill. Negotiators refused to provide a doctor—who might become another prisoner—and the gunmen freed one hostage. Meanwhile, the SAS and Metro officers inserted cameras and microphones through the

Special Air Service commandos prepare to enter the Iranian embassy in London. The commandos successfully freed the 25 remaining hostages, killed five of the terrorists, and captured one. (*AFP/Getty Images*)

embassy's walls and down chimneys and planted other listening devices inside packages of food delivered to the gunmen. That covert surveillance revealed that the terrorists occupied three of the building's five floors, holding their captives in two rooms.

Hostage negotiators stalled the gunmen as their deadline passed, and the standoff dragged on for six days. At one point, officers agreed to broadcast the terrorists' message worldwide, prompting release of two more captives. Police kept their word, but reporters misquoted part of the message, producing more furious threats. On May 5 the invaders murdered hostage Abbas Lavasani and tossed his body out the embassy's front door, with a promise to kill one more victim every half-hour until their demands were met.

SAS officers launched their assault with seven minutes to spare. Descending on ropes from the embassy's roof, they penetrated upstairs windows and hammered through walls, hurling flash-bang grenades and firing tear-gas canisters, then killing five of the terrorists who still brandished weapons. The sixth invader dropped his gun and was captured alive. None of the 25 surviving hostages were injured.

In retrospect, while deadly force was finally employed to end the siege, the SAS and Metro officers considered the standoff a victory for hostage negotiators who had delayed the impending murder of the other captives and bought time for the assault troops to refine their entry strategy.

HOSTAGE-TAKERS

Every law enforcement officer dreads hostage situations, which place innocent persons at risk both from felons and from the police sent to free them. Some such incidents occur spontaneously, as grim accidents, while others are planned out for months in advance, to promote a specific goal. In any case, hostage-takers always want something, demanding compliance in return for safe release of their captives. It is a negotiator's job to find out what the hostage-takers want and how authorities may best resolve the siege without bloodshed.

Hostage situations generally fall into four broad categories. Domestic conflicts such as the siege that claimed the life of LAPD Officer Randal Simmons in February 2008 arise from quarrels between relatives or friends that escalate into violence and end with one or more subjects threatening others. Such incidents are rarely planned, though some cases involving child-custody disputes or failed romances may include some planning. Extreme emotion in these cases may limit demands, and SWAT has no authority to settle issues reserved for family courts.

Workplace incidents arise from a personal grievance on the hostage-taker's part against employers or coworkers. Armed invasion of a work-place commonly includes a greater number of hostages than is found in a normal household, and frequently involves a larger target area than the average home. Demands in such cases often include reinstatement of fired employees, back pay or other benefits, and/or apologies for perceived insults.

Other personal incidents, such as the February 1977 standoff with Anthony Kiritsis, are similar to workplace incidents but gener-ally spring from grievances against persons or companies whom the hostage-taker believes have abused him. Kiritsis targeted a mortgage broker he blamed for the loss of his home. Other targets in such cases may include insurance companies (for denial of claims), financial insti-tutions (for rejecting loan applications, etc.), schools (in disputes over grades or some disciplinary action), or even media outlets (if the sub-ject feels that he has been maligned). Again, demands normally focus on compensation or a public apology.

Unintended hostage situations nearly always involve subjects involved in some other crime, such as armed robbery or carjacking, who are surprised by the arrival of authorities before they flee the scene. Demands in such cases commonly include money and a safe means of escape—an aircraft, armored car, etc.—with a promise to release hos-tages when the subject arrives in a safe location. Most law enforcement agencies automatically refuse any demands for unconditional freedom, as they do demands for weapons, drugs, and liquor, but despite well-known bans on such negotiations, criminals still try to talk their way out of tight corners.

Terrorist incidents, like the embassy seizure in London, are normally the best-planned and most widely publicized cases of hos-tage seizure. One of the first such incidents occurred in November

1532, when Spanish soldiers led by Francisco Pizarro captured Atahualpa, king of the Incas, in Peru. Pizarro demanded a ransom in
gold equivalent to $170 million, which the Incas delivered after five
months of negotiation. Even then, the Spaniards broke their word
and executed Atahualpa in July 1533. The first barricade-and-hostage
situation occurred in August 1896, when Armenian rebels seized a
bank in Constantinople, Turkey. Authorities met their demands for
ransom and freedom, then slaughtered 6,000 innocent Armenians in
retaliation.[2]

The late 1960s introduced America and the world at large to wide-
spread terrorist operations, including numerous airline hijackings and
the OPEC raid of December 1975, when six extremists led by Illich
"Carlos the Jackal" Ramirez seized 70 hostages at the Austrian headquarters of the Organization of Petroleum Exporting Countries. After
a failed police assault that left three persons dead and five wounded,
authorities agreed to release the terrorists with 33 hostages and grant
them safe passage to Algeria.[3]

That incident, and others like it, prompted most countries to adopt
a public "zero tolerance" attitude toward negotiation with hostage-
takers, at least where freedom is concerned, but incidents continue to
the present day. Notorious cases include the following:

- *December 24, 1999:* Five Pakistanis hijacked Indian Airlines Flight
  814, en route from Katmandu, Nepal, to Delhi, India. After fatally
  stabbing one passenger, the terrorists diverted the aircraft to
  Afghanistan, where the hijackers freed their hostages in exchange
  for the release of three imprisoned Muslim extremists.
- *April 12, 2002:* Members of the Revolutionary Armed Forces of
  Colombia (FARC) kidnapped 12 politicians in the state of Valle
  del Cauca, threatening to execute them if the government did not
  withdraw troops from areas claimed by the rebels. The government refused, and fruitless negotiations dragged on until June
  2007, when the FARC announced that 11 of the hostages had been
  killed during failed rescue attempts. Authorities denied any such
  efforts. The last surviving hostage was released in February 2009.
  He explained that FARC members had mistaken some of their

ALTA VIEW HOSPITAL (1991)

Shortly after midnight on September 20, 1991, 39-year-old Richard Worthington entered Alta View Hospital in Sandy, Utah. Armed with a shotgun, a pistol, and several sticks of dynamite, Worthington hoped to kill Dr. Glade Curtis, who had performed a tubal ligation on Worthington's wife. Worthington had agreed to the sterilization surgery after his eighth child was born, but later regretted his choice. The hospital canceled Worthington's bill in return for his promise not to file a lawsuit, but he sank into depression, brooding and dreaming of revenge.

On arrival at the hospital, Worthington saw Dr. Curtis's car in the parking lot and vandalized it, then left a homemade bomb in a nearby flower bed. Invading Alta View's Women's Health Center, Worthington missed Dr. Curtis (who hid in his office and telephoned police), but he shot and killed nurse Karla Roth when she tried to disarm him. Next, he seized six hostages, including two nurses, expectant mother Christan Downey, her husband, and two newborn infants.

own comrades for government troops in 2007, and killed the other hostages before recognizing their error. The kidnappers remain unidentified.

○ *October 23, 2002:* During Russia's second war with rebel forces in Chechnya, Chechen terrorists invaded Moscow's Nord-Ost theater, seizing 850 hostages and demanding the immediate withdrawal of Russian troops from Chechnya. Members of Russia's Spetznaz ("Special Forces") team assaulted the theater on October 26, flooding it with toxic gas before they entered. At least 129 hostages and 33 terrorists died in the assault (some reports claim 204 deaths), and 700 hostages were injured, with some left permanently disabled. Officials blamed all of the deaths and injuries on the gas used by Spetznaz.[4]

The Alta Vista siege lasted for 18 hours, during which time Christan Downey gave birth to a daughter, Caitlin. At one point, Worthington sent a hostage outside to retrieve his crude bomb, which kept SWAT officers at bay. Two negotiators from the Salt Lake City Police Department, Sergeant Don Bell and Detective Jill Candland, used their skills to draw Worthington back from the brink of violence, while hunger and depression wore him down. At 5:45 P.M., Worthington agreed to surrender, emerging with some of his hostages to face arrest.

At trial, Richard Worthington pled guilty to Karla Roth's murder and received a 35-year prison term. Defense attorneys later argued that his mind had been unbalanced by the stand-off and his plea was thus invalid, but appellate courts rejected that claim. After several failed escape attempts and bungled efforts to commit suicide, Worthington hanged himself in his prison cell on November 11, 1993. By then, his case had been dramatized in a made-for-television movie, *Deliver Them From Evil: The Taking of Alta View*, starring actors Harry Hamlin and Teri Garr.

- *September 1, 2004:* In another incident spawned by Russia's Second Chechen War, terrorists seized a school at Beslan in the North Caucasus region of Russia, demanding concessions in return for safe release of 1,100 hostages. Spetznaz troops stormed the school on September 3, producing another massacre. At least 385 persons died in the attack, including 334 hostages (186 of them children), and another 783 were wounded. As in Moscow, some reports cite higher numbers of injured and dead.[5]
- *July 19, 2007:* Taliban extremists captured 23 South Korean missionaries in Afghanistan, executing two before the others were released in late August. In return for their freedom, South Korea's government agreed to withdraw its force of 200 soldiers from Afghanistan, where a coalition led by the United States has engaged

in antiterrorist operations since October 2001. Taliban spokesmen claim that they also received a ransom payment of $20 million, which remains unconfirmed.

STANDOFF

While every hostage situation is unique, all proceed through definable phases.[6] The initial phase is usually brief and often violent, as criminals invade their target and seize control. Whether or not a standoff is intended, the authorities arrive, surround the site, and receive demands.

The second phase, negotiation, begins with the arrival of one or more officers authorized to discuss terms with the barricaded subjects. Most agencies forbid freeing the subjects and/or providing them with weapons or intoxicating substances that make the standoff more dangerous for all concerned. However, those restrictions do not bar negotiators from promising things that they may not deliver. Because hostage negotiators work under close supervision, they can often stall a subject's deadlines by appealing for time to consult their superiors.

A negotiator's first priority is collecting information about the hostage-takers and their captives. How many subjects are involved? How many captives are they holding? Are the hostage-takers mentally unbalanced or intoxicated? Are they "ordinary" felons, or terrorists pursuing an extremist agenda? Are they seeking "suicide by cop"? Are any of the hostages wounded or suffering from ailments that require medication? Answers to those questions, if available, help SWAT plan a solution to the crisis while the negotiator builds a psychological profile of his opponents.

Whenever possible, hostage negotiators work in teams, including a primary and a secondary negotiator.[7] The primary negotiator is the team's mouthpiece, conducting all discussions with the barricaded subject, while his backup listens, observes, and provides suggestions as needed. Regardless of personal training and skill, no negotiator is perfect. Anyone may run short of ideas in a crisis, whereupon the secondary negotiator provides assistance—sometimes aided by psychologists, ministers, or persons acquainted with the subject who possess important private information.

Despite some grim exceptions—such as the FBI's 1993 siege of the Branch Davidian compound at Waco, Texas—the likelihood of bloodshed declines as hostage crises are protracted. For that reason, negotiators are trained to prolong standoffs, pushing back a subject's deadlines. Negotiators prefer open-ended questions to those with yes-or-no answers; they distract subjects with details about their escape (what type of aircraft is preferred, etc.) and sidetrack them whenever possible with personal discussions that stall for time and give authorities more information about the situation.[8]

At the same time, a negotiator must avoid angering the subject, who may react by punishing the hostages. Safe release of captives is the negotiator's primary goal, which may include persuading hostage-takers to permit medical treatment of ill or wounded captives. Ideally, a negotiator may persuade the subject to release some of his prisoners, either for health reasons or as a trade-off for concessions from authorities. In the 1980 London siege, terrorists freed two hostages in return for the televised broadcast of their demands. In other cases, hostages have been exchanged for food, or when negotiators convinced subjects to release women and children as a show of "good faith." Terrorists who target members of a certain group may also agree to release hostages of other races, religions, or nationalities.

Above all else, hostage negotiators seek to maintain calm, while establishing relationships between themselves and barricaded subjects. They avoid arguments and are trained to avoid saying "no" to any demand, preferring evasive discussions and bids for more time. Counteroffers are standard procedure, deflecting a demand for freedom with offers to contact a subject's family or friends, to provide more food, adjust the heat or air-conditioning, and so on. Negotiators always strive for a positive, upbeat attitude, while encouraging subjects to view their captives as human beings rather than pawns in a dangerous game.[9]

DEAL/NO DEAL

Hostage-takers often launch negotiations with impossible demands: weapons and drugs, vast sums of cash, or release of imprisoned felons in foreign countries where SWAT has no jurisdiction. Negotiators stall for time and counter with minor concessions. And while most nations now claim "zero tolerance" toward negotiation with terrorists, there are occasional exceptions.

A case in point occurred in June 1985, when Muslim extremists hijacked TWA Flight 847 en route from Athens to Rome with 153 passengers and eight crew members aboard. They diverted the plane to Beirut, then Algiers, where the gunmen issued demands, including the release of 766 Muslims jailed in Israel, plus international condemnation of Israeli and American actions in the Middle East. Despite a strict

STOCKHOLM SYNDROME

Stockholm syndrome is a psychological condition sometimes seen in hostages and kidnapping victims. Victims suffering from this disorder display sympathy and loyalty toward their abductors after they are rescued. In some cases, the victims argue that the hostage-takers should be freed from custody, and some even display romantic attraction to those who victimized them.

The syndrome draws its name from an incident that occurred in Stockholm, Sweden, during August 1973. Bandits tried to rob a local bank and were surprised in the act by police, sparking a standoff spanning six days. After the robbers surrendered, several of their captives displayed emotional attachment to them and spoke out publicly in their defense. Since that time, other notorious cases of alleged Stockholm syndrome have included the following:

★ *February 1974:* Members of the Symbionese Liberation Army kidnapped millionaire heiress Patricia Hearst and held her for ransom, then apparently converted her to active membership in their organization. Despite annihilation of the gang's leadership in Los Angeles, and frequent opportunities for escape, Hearst remained with her captors until she was arrested by FBI agents. At trial for bank robbery in 1976, Hearst offered a "brain-washing" defense but was convicted and sentenced to 35 years in prison, later reduced to seven years.

"no-negotiation" policy, discussions proceeded. All but one of the hostages—a U.S. Navy diver murdered by the terrorists—were released by June 30. Over the next several weeks, Israel freed all 766 of the Muslim inmates, while denying that their release was linked to the hijacking. One of the terrorists was captured in Germany, in 1987, and served an eight-year prison term. Another suspect died in a February 2008 car bombing allegedly carried out by Israeli commandos. Three others are still at large.[10]

★ *May 1977:* Serial sex offender Cameron Hooker and his wife kidnapped hitchhiker Colleen Stan in California, holding her captive until 1984. Hooker forced Stan to sign a "slave contract," allegedly binding her to a nationwide criminal organization, but he later granted her limited freedom, including unsupervised visits to her parents' home. At Hooker's trial, where he received a 104-year prison sentence, Stan testified that she lived in fear of Hooker's threats to kill her family if she did not return to him on command. Defense attorneys failed to convince jurors that her captivity was voluntary.

★ *March 1998:* Austrian felon Wolfgang Priklopil kidnapped 10-year-old Natascha Kampusch and held her prisoner for eight years, until she finally escaped. Free once more, Kampusch grieved upon learning that Priklopil had killed himself to avoid arrest.

★ *June 2002:* Utah resident Elizabeth Smart, age 14, was snatched from her home by members of a polygamist cult led by Brian "Emmanuel" Mitchell. After a period of close captivity, when she was bound to trees, Smart traveled with the cult through California and Nevada, where she claimed to be Mitchell's daughter. When spotted by Utah police, nine months after her kidnapping, Smart initially lied about her age and claimed to be one of Mitchell's wives.

SWAT team members take a suspect into custody after a nearly six-hour hostage and standoff situation. *(AP Photo/*Foster's Daily Democrat, *Craig Osborne)*

Hostage situations may be resolved in one of three ways. In rare cases, like that of TWA Flight 847, criminal demands are granted (with or without official denials), and the hostage-takers escape. Another option is direct assault, which may liberate the hostages without injury or produce a disaster, as in the Russian cases cited above. The third, ideal resolution occurs when barricaded subjects surrender peacefully and are taken into custody.

BECOMING A HOSTAGE NEGOTIATOR

Hollywood often entices young people to seek careers in law enforcement. FBI applications increased greatly after *The Silence of the Lambs* (1991) depicted rookie agent Clarisse Starling pursuing serial killers "Buffalo Bill" and Hannibal "The Cannibal" Lecter; but in fact, FBI profilers do not hunt killers in the field. Likewise, while films such as *The Negotiator* (1998) and *Hostage* (2005) portray hostage negotiation as a grand adventure, reality is very different.

First, as with membership in SWAT teams, all would-be negotiators must first "pay their dues" as rank-and-file members of law enforcement, then display special aptitude that makes them suited for a difficult job. To become a SWAT negotiator, applicants must, of course, first qualify for a SWAT team. Having cleared that hurdle, applicants must still observe and learn.

Various training courses exist for hostage negotiators, including those offered by different police academies or by the Public Agency Training Council and Midwest Police Consultants.[11] In 2003 the Federal Law Enforcement Training Center and the International Association of Chiefs of Police joined forces to produce a *Hostage Negotiation Study Guide* that covers the subject effectively, but no amount of reading or classroom instruction can take the place of actual experience.

Individuals who feel that a career in hostage negotiation might suit them should obtain a solid education in psychology—including abnormal or deviant psychology—then join a law enforcement agency that includes hostage negotiators, fulfill all responsibilities on an excellent level, and hope for the best. As with other SWAT duties, training and on-the-job education never end.

Controversial Cases

Fairfax, Virginia

Dr. Salvatore Culosi was a respected optometrist, admired by his patients, well liked by his neighbors. Unknown to those patients and neighbors, however, Culosi had a sideline in illegal gambling, handling bets on sporting events. Beginning in mid-2005, an undercover officer with the Fairfax County Police Department placed multiple bets with Culosi, recording the transactions as evidence for criminal charges.

On the night of January 24, 2006, the officer drove to Culosi's home and met the doctor outside. He placed one final bet, then signaled his backup team to make the arrest. Two SWAT team members advanced with guns drawn, and something went terribly wrong. Instead of simply arresting the unarmed suspect, Officer Deval Bullock fired a .45-caliber pistol slug into Culosi's chest and killed the doctor where he stood.

What went wrong? In an interview with Internal Affairs, Officer Bullock said that he received the signal to advance while seated in a nearby car. As he got out, his gun hand bumped the car's door, causing it to "involuntarily make a fist and depress the trigger." Still, he said, the shooting was Culosi's fault, because the doctor "began to exhibit the characteristics of someone who was going to run" when he saw the SWAT officers approaching.[1]

Dr. Culosi's family and other critics of the shooting questioned why SWAT was summoned to make the arrest at all, since Culosi had no criminal record, had never engaged in any violent acts, and was not known to own firearms. An official report, issued a year after the shooting, noted that Officer Bullock himself "was not comfortable with the original plan and challenged it prior to the briefing." The *Washington Post* declared that in Culosi's case, "SWAT team power was unnecessary. Risk assessment policies have been inconsistent and are being revised."[2]

Although the fatal shooting was an accident, it could not be excused. SWAT officers are trained to carry their guns in a "ready" position, without touching the trigger unless they intend to fire. Violation of that rule, resulting in death, cost Officer Bullock a three-week suspension without pay, but neither side was satisfied with that disciplinary action.

Officer Marshall Thielen, president of the local police officers' union, told reporters, "The discipline is very disproportionate to prior cases. This was a case where an officer was trying to do everything right, with good intentions. I feel the punishment may be politically motivated because of all the media attention." Culosi's parents, meanwhile, wanted Officer Bullock dismissed from his job. "Any sanction short of this," they said, "we consider to be nothing more than permission to go out once again and have the opportunity to unjustly kill."[3]

COPS AND CRITICS

Police are constantly immersed in controversy over use of force in their communities. As human beings, all are capable of error and emotion that lead to some unfortunate results. Their training—more intense for SWAT than officers in any other role—is meant to mold professionals and ward off accidental tragedies, but negligence and some deliberate brutality is still a fact of life. All occupations have "bad apples," and police work—with its round-the-clock exposure to violence, crime, and corruption—causes more personal problems than most.

Critics of SWAT seldom suggest that special teams should not exist for crisis situations. Neither do they argue that police are *always* able to avoid the use of deadly force. Rather, most critics claim that SWAT is used too often, and in situations that do not require application of special weapons and tactics.

In August 1999 the nonpartisan Cato Institute—pledged "to increase the understanding of public policies based on the principles of limited

MOVE (1985)

The Movement Toward a More Christian Life—better known simply as MOVE—was founded in 1972 by Pennsylvania residents Donald Glassey and Vinvent Leaphart (who called himself "John Africa"). The group, consisting almost entirely of African Americans who adopted the last name "Africa," proposed a "back-to-nature" lifestyle and condemned modern technology. Ironically, instead of moving to the open countryside, they colonized the heart of Philadelphia's ghetto and promoted their message through loudspeakers in their compound, blaring MOVE's message to unhappy neighbors around the clock. Other complaints included claims of unhealthy living conditions, children withheld from school, MOVE dogs running wild around the neighborhood, and alleged petty crimes committed by various compound residents.

Local police were frequently at odds with MOVE over the numerous complaints, while spokesmen for the group—described in some reports as a religious cult—accused authorities of racist discrimination. MOVE's first residence was besieged by police for much of 1978, which climaxed with an August SWAT raid that left Officer James Ramp slain by gunfire, while seven other officers, five firefighters, three MOVE members, and three bystanders were injured. Jurors convicted nine

government, free markets, individual liberty, and peace"[4]—published a report on SWAT by Diane Weber, titled *Warrior Cops: The Ominous Growth of Paramilitarism in American Police Departments.* Another Cato Institute report, Radley Balko's *Overkill: The Rise of Paramilitary Police Raids in America*, appeared in July 2006. Balko summarizes the view of most SWAT critics in the foreword to his report:

> Over the last 25 years, America has seen a disturbing militarization of its civilian law enforcement, along with a dramatic and unsettling rise in the use of paramilitary police units . . . for

MOVE members of third-degree murder in Officer Ramp's case, and they received 30-year prison terms.[5]

Following that incident, MOVE relocated to a larger residence and resumed its disruptive activities. Police made their second attempt to silence the group on May 13, 1985, but the initial raid went awry when an officer was shot, saved from serious injury by his body armor. A short time later, airborne SWAT officers dropped a four-pound charge of plastic explosives on the roof of MOVE's fortified headquarters. The resultant explosion and fire killed John Africa and 10 followers, five of them children. From MOVE's encampment the fire swiftly spread, destroying more than 50 nearby homes owned by persons with no connection to MOVE.[6]

Officials defended the bombing while publicly mourning the scope of the damage. MOVE survivors sued those responsible and won their case in June 1996, when a federal jury ordered the City of Philadelphia, ex-Police Commissioner George Sambor, and ex-Fire Commissioner William Richmond to pay $1.5 million in damages for use of excessive force. Trial testimony demonstrated that Sambor and Richmond were both at the scene of the bombing and that they ordered firefighters to let the blaze burn. Prior to that trial, other bombing survivors had collected more than $27 million from the city government.[7]

routine police work. The most common use of SWAT teams today is to serve narcotics warrants, usually with forced, unannounced entry into the home.

These increasingly frequent raids, 40,000 per year by one estimate, are needlessly subjecting nonviolent drug offenders, bystanders, and wrongly targeted civilians to the terror of having their homes invaded while they're sleeping, usually by teams of heavily armed paramilitary units dressed not as police officers but as soldiers. These raids bring unnecessary violence and provocation to nonviolent drug offenders, many of whom were guilty of only misdemeanors. The raids terrorize innocents when police mistakenly target the wrong residence. And they have resulted in dozens of needless deaths and injuries, not only of drug offenders, but also of police officers, children, bystanders, and innocent suspects.[8]

Critics also argue that the federal government makes matters worse by furnishing local police with military weapons, vehicles, and other equipment which, in Balko's terms, produces "a more confrontational, militaristic approach" to crime-fighting than most situations warrant.[9] As a result, the critics say, violence escalates, endangering police, unarmed suspects, and innocent bystanders.

Incidents cited to prove the critics' case include the following:

- *November 1991*: SWAT officers in DeKalb County, Georgia, staged a "no-knock" raid on the home of suspected drug dealer Xavier Bennett at 2:30 A.M. Awakened by the sound of smashing doors, Bennett rushed from his bedroom with a gun, whereupon officers accidentally shot and killed his eight-year-old stepson. Police jailed Bennett for cocaine possession. No disciplinary action resulted from the child's death.

- *November 1993*: In a similar incident, officers in Houston, Texas, staged an early-morning no-knock raid at the home of Edward Benavides, who woke in a panic and fatally shot Officer Leslie Early, then surrendered when he recognized the home-invaders as police. One policeman told the *Houston Chronicle,* "I think the Task Force may have had more to do with getting [Officer Early] killed than the kid [Benavides] did," but jurors convicted Benavides of murder and he received a life sentence in 1994.[10]

- *September 1998*: SWAT officers in Charlotte, North Carolina, staged a no-knock drug raid at the home of Robert Hardin, killing innocent visitor Charles Potts with four gunshots. Hardin and another guest told reporters they thought the house was being robbed. "Only thing I heard was a big boom," Hardin said. "The lights went off and then they came back on . . . [and] everybody reacted."[11] Again, no disciplinary action resulted.

- *September 2000*: SWAT officers killed Lynette Jackson during a no-knock raid on her home in Riverdale, Georgia. The previous month, Jackson's home had been robbed, and police who answered that call found a small bag of cocaine belonging to Jackson's boyfriend. No charges were filed, but the September raiders hoped to find more. Jackson had purchased a gun since the burglary, and it cost her her life when officers burst into her home. A neighbor said, "I think she was scared and she probably thought it was another break-in."[12]

- *February 2001*: Edwin Delamora, his wife, and their two children were sleeping at home in Del Valle, Texas, when officers stormed the dwelling with battering rams. While his wife dialed 911 for help, Delamora fired through the door, killing Officer Keith Ruiz. Surviving raiders found a small quantity of drugs in the house, and Delamora received a life sentence for murder. Police later said they were sent to the home by tips from an anonymous informer.

- *December 2001*: Officers from the same task force that killed Edwin Delamora staged a no-knock raid at the home of teenage drug suspect Tony Martinez in Travis County, Texas. Martinez, who had no criminal record, was sleeping on the couch when raiders burst in. He sat up, startled, and was killed by a shot to the chest. Although Martinez was unarmed, the raiders were not disciplined.

- *April 2002*: A SWAT team equipped with a helicopter raided Jose Colon's home in Bellport, New York. Roused from sleep by the chopper overhead, Colon emerged to face officers rushing across his lawn. One of the SWAT officers stumbled and accidentally fired three shots from a submachine gun, killing Colon. Eight ounces of marijuana, found in the house, produced an official ruling of justifiable homicide.

- *October 2002*: SWAT officers raided a home in Windsor, Pennsylvania, seeking drugs, and shot unarmed houseguest Meredith Sutherland Jr. as he sat up in bed. Sutherland survived his wounds, after spending 11 days in a coma and three weeks in the hospital. Other occupants of the home were held on drug charges.

WACO (1993)

The Branch Davidian sect was created in 1955 from a rift in the Seventh-Day Adventist Church. Members settled on a hill outside Waco, Texas, which they called Mount Carmel, after a mountain mentioned in the Old Testament. By 1983 the sect was dominated by Vernon Howell (1959–93), known to his followers as "David Koresh." In March 1986 Howell announced a switch to polygamous marriage, claiming the personal right to 140 wives. He never reached that number, though, as total membership—including men and children—only topped 100 near the end of 1992.

By then, Howell and his faithful were in trouble. First, in 1987, they tried to kill a rival "prophet" who denied Howell's claims that he could raise the dead. No one died in that clash, but Howell and several others were charged with attempted murder. Jurors acquitted them all at trial.

In May 1992 ATF agents received information that Howell's group was stockpiling illegal weapons, including grenades and machine guns. They also heard tales of child abuse, which fell outside of ATF jurisdiction. On February 28, 1993, members of the ATF's Special Response Team stormed Mount Carmel, but the raid went badly. Four agents and six Davidians died in the skirmish, while others on both sides were wounded before the ATF retreated.[13]

Members of the FBI's Hostage Rescue Team then took control at Mount Carmel for a siege lasting 51 days. During those weeks, hostage negotiators secured the safe release of 19 children. Then, around 6:00 A.M. on April 19, 1993, FBI agents in armored vehicles approached the sect's fortified compound to flood it with tear gas. No one emerged before 12:07 P.M., when

- *February 2004*: Raiders stormed the Middletown, Pennsylvania, home of James Hoskins, seeking to arrest his brother on drug charges. As Hoskins rose from bed, nude and unarmed, one officer shot him, resulting in loss of a leg. Hoskins and his girlfriend

witnesses saw flames leaping amidst the buildings. The fire spread quickly, then burned itself out roughly an hour later. In the ashes, FBI agents found Vernon Howell and 75 others dead, including two pregnant women and 21 children.[14]

After much confusion and angry debate in Texas and Washington, D.C., 12 Davidian survivors faced trial for conspiring to kill federal agents. Jurors in their two-month trial acquitted seven on all counts and convicted five on reduced charges of aiding and abetting murder. They received 40-year prison terms, later reduced on appeal, and all were freed by July 2007. Terrorist Timothy McVeigh bombed Oklahoma City's federal building on April 19, 1995, to honor the dead at Waco.

Smoking fire consumes the Branch Davidian compound during the FBI Hostage Rescue Team's assault to end the 51-day standoff with cult leader Vernon Howell (known as David Koresh) and his followers. (*Greg Smith/Corbis*)

both insist the raiders never identified themselves as police. His brother was later jailed for possessing "a small amount of marijuana, a glass pipe, and about $622." Police declined to investigate the shooting.[15]

o *January 2005*: SWAT officers raided the Baltimore, Maryland, home of Cheryl Noel after detectives found marijuana seeds and traces of cocaine in her family's trash can outside. Noel, armed with a legally registered gun since her step-daughter's murder years earlier, bolted from her bedroom as officers kicked in her doors. Shot three times at close range, Noel died instantly. While her family filed a fruitless lawsuit, police rewarded her killer with a medal for "bravery, courage and valor."[16]

o *August 2005*: SWAT raiders struck the Sunrise, Florida, home of bartender Anthony Diotaiuto at 6:00 A.M., catching him asleep after his normal night shift. Officers shot Diotaiuto 10 times as he emerged from his bedroom, afterward seizing two ounces of marijuana and scales allegedly used to weigh drugs. Next-door neighbor Rudy Strauss told reporters that the raiders stormed Diotaiuto's apartment without identifying themselves.

o *September 2005*: SWAT officers stormed the wrong house in Stockbridge, Georgia, using battering rams and flash-bang grenades before dragging Roy and Belinda Baker outside in their underwear. Police Chief Russ Abernathy admitted that the raiders meant to arrest a next-door neighbor, calling the mistake "inexcusable" and "not acceptable," but he imposed no discipline and said no-knock raids would continue after "reviewing procedures" were completed.[17]

o *March 2006*: Another Georgia no-knock raid, this one in Macon, cost the life of Officer Joseph Whitehead when occupants of the home woke from sleep and fired shots at figures they mistook for neighborhood gang members. Despite the local sheriff's admission that "It just went wrong," both occupants of the house faced death-penalty charges for killing a policeman. No trial date had been scheduled as of spring 2009.[18]

o *December 2007*: Body armor saved the lives of two SWAT officers in Minneapolis, Minnesota, after a 30-member team raided the wrong address in search of drugs. Innocent homeowner Vang Khang fired two shotgun blasts when raiders burst into his home, then somehow avoided injury from a storm of automatic fire. Next-door neighbor Ruth Hayes told *USA Today*, "I must've heard over 20 or 30 shots, I swear, it was scary. . . . It was crazy. It was just like havoc."[19] Admitting their near-fatal mistake, police filed no charges against Vang Khang.

○ *July 2008*: A sheriff's SWAT team raided the home of Mayor Cheye Calvo in Berwyn Heights, Maryland, after Calvo allegedly received a 32-pound package of marijuana addressed to his wife. As usual in such raids, officers stormed the house while its occupants slept, fatally shooting the mayor's two dogs and grilling the family for hours in custody. Subsequent reports announced that the Calvos were innocent. Police jailed two other suspects who conspired to smuggle drugs in parcels addressed to innocent persons, then steal them prior to delivery. An FBI investigation of the raid was planned, but no results have been published.

ROOM FOR IMPROVEMENT

Any task performed by human beings may result in failure that is sometimes tragic, and constructive suggestions for improvement are always welcome. Radley Balko and the Cato Institute propose the following solutions to SWAT's worst problems:[20]

1. End giveaways and sale of Pentagon military equipment, designed and purchased for use in foreign combat against hostile armies.
2. Set a good example for local police at the national level by avoiding incidents such as the 1992 Ruby Ridge incident and the 1993 Waco siege.
3. Remove the U.S. military and federal agencies from enforcement of local laws, since their existing oversight procedures are less rigorous than those established by many local police departments.
4. Return SWAT to its original function, limiting call-outs to cases where innocent lives are endangered by barricaded criminals or terrorists, leaving routine arrests, raids and crowd-control functions to other law enforcement units.
5. Pass new laws establishing a right to home defense, thus banning prosecution of innocent persons who use force against unidentified home-invaders.

6. Impose strict liability on agencies and officers who raid the wrong address or use deadly force against innocent persons, including both criminal and civil (financial) penalties.
7. Tighten search warrant standards to eliminate anonymous informants and false leads delivered to police for monetary rewards or other favors, such as reduction of an informer's own criminal charges.
8. Increase transparency of police operations by videotaping all SWAT raids and making those tapes available to the public, thus eliminating any risk of cover-ups.
9. Establish civilian review boards to deal with complaints of police misconduct, rather than allowing a department to investigate and "clear" itself.
10. Eliminate intimidation of innocent victims in wrong-address raids, documented in some cases as a means of preventing lawsuits.
11. Expand accountability for official misconduct to those who issue illegal orders, type the wrong address on search warrants, and so on, to emphatically discourage negligence and remove repeat offenders from their jobs.

Police commonly oppose all of those suggestions, deeming them radical steps proposed by civilians who do not understand the rigors of front-line law enforcement.

While that view may be accurate, to some extent, any challenge to increased discipline and public oversight also makes the complaining agencies *seem* guilty of trying to conceal misconduct.

SWAT
International

Munich, West Germany

At 4:30 A.M. on September 5, 1972, eight members of the Palestinian terrorist group Black September invaded the compound where hundreds of athletes slept, resting before another day of the Olympic Games. Dressed in tracksuits and carrying guns and grenades in duffel bags, the prowlers used stolen keys to invade two apartments occupied by Israeli athletes. After killing a weightlifter and wounding one coach, they captured 11 hostages as several more escaped through windows to alert police.

While the terrorists demanded freedom for 234 Palestinians jailed in Israel, plus two criminals held in West Germany, Munich police surrounded the Olympic Village. None had any special training in counterterrorist operations, and five designated snipers were chosen because they enjoyed target shooting on weekends. One of them later told investigators, "I am of the opinion that I am not a sharpshooter."[1] That lack of skill soon proved disastrous.

During negotiations with authorities, the gunmen killed a second hostage, then demanded safe passage with their captives to Egypt. German officials agreed, providing two helicopters that carried the gunmen and nine hostages to a nearby military airport. There, a Boeing 727 waited, with German police disguised as crew members. The helicopters landed at 10:30 P.M., and the terrorists soon recognized the trap. A police sniper fired at the kidnap team's leader and missed, setting off a

The two West German border police helicopters that carried armed terrorists and their nine Israeli hostages stand at an air force base 20 miles west of Munich on September 7, 1972. The helicopter in the foreground is a burned-out shell as a result of a hand grenade explosion set off by one of the terrorists apparently committing suicide rather than risking capture. (*Associated Press*)

chaotic battle that claimed the lives of all nine hostages, five of the kidnappers, and a policeman inside the airport's control tower.

Munich police were harshly criticized for their handling of the Olympic Village incident. Israeli spokesmen claimed that West Germany rejected offers of help from specially trained commandos, while West German officials denied that any such offer was made. Israel subsequently hunted down and killed various Arab militants suspected of planning the raid, a campaign dramatized in the movie *Munich* (2005).

SWAT GOES GLOBAL

The Munich massacre and other acts of terrorism in the early 1970s encouraged the creation of SWAT-type units throughout Europe and the world at large. Between September 1972 and April 1973, special counterterrorist teams were created in Austria, Belgium, Denmark, Finland, France, and West Germany. In 1974 Italy created its Central Security Operations Service. Norway organized its Delta team in 1976, followed by Japan's Special Assault Team the following year. Six new units appeared in 1978, including Australia's Special Response and Security team, Brazil's Special Police Operations Battalion, Greece's Special Anti-Terrorist Unit, Ireland's Emergency Response Unit, Italy's Special Intervention Group, Serbia's Special Anti-Terrorist Unit, and Spain's Special Operations Group. The decade ended with creation of Russia's Special Purpose Police Squad and Sweden's Piketen unit in 1979.

SWAT units continued to spread in the 1980s, with creation of a second team in Norway, plus new units in Iceland, India, the Philippines, Portugal, Sri Lanka, Taiwan, and Thailand. The 1990s saw special response units organized in Albania, Argentina, Colombia, Croatia, Estonia, Latvia, Malaysia, Pakistan, and Sweden (the National Task Force). Units created since 2000 include the Rapid Action Battalion in Bangladesh, China's Snow Wolf Commando Unit, and a second Serbian team, the Counter-Terrorist Unit.

GSG-9

The Munich tragedy, coupled with bombings and murders committed by the Red Army Faction (RAF), a leftist terrorist group also known as the Baader-Meinhof Gang. prompted the German Federal Police to create a new special response group in April 1973. It was called *Grenzschutzgruppe* ("Border Guard Group") 9, shortened to GSG-9. The group's organization and training were patterned after Israel's General Staff Reconnaissance Unit, created in 1957 to combat terrorists.

Like SWAT in the United States, GSG-9 serves multiple functions. The team is called to deal with acts of terrorism, kidnapping and hostage-taking, pursuit of dangerous fugitives, and certain cases of extortion. According to the Federal Police Web site, GSG-9 was deployed more than 1,500 times between 1973 and 2003, using deadly force on only five occasions.[2] While details for many of its call-outs remain secret, those known publicly include the following:

- *Operation Fire Magic*: In October 1977 four Arab terrorists hijacked Lufthansa Flight 181 with 86 persons aboard and diverted it from Germany to Mogadishu, Somalia, where they demanded release of imprisoned RAF members. On the night of October 17, GSG-9 officers stormed the grounded aircraft at Mogadishu International Airport, killing three gunmen and wounding the fourth. No hostages were harmed.
- *June 1993*: GSG-9 officers captured RAF terrorist Birgit Hogefeld in Bad Kleinen, Germany. Her companion, Wolfgang Grams, killed Officer Michael Newrzella, then suffered fatal gunshot wounds. Police say that Grams shot himself, while RAF supporters claim he was murdered in retaliation for shooting Officer Newrzella.
- *August 1993*: Without firing a shot, GSG-9 captured a gunman who hijacked a KLM flight from Tunis to Amsterdam. No hostages were injured.
- *March 1999*: GSG-9 arrested Metin Kaplan, a Turkish immigrant known as the "Caliph of Cologne," on charges of killing a rival Muslim activist. Kaplan was convicted of hiring the killers and spent four years in prison.
- *April 2004*: Assigned to protect German diplomats in Iraq, two GSG-9 officers died in a terrorist ambush near Fallujah, while escorting embassy personnel. The attackers later apologized, saying they mistook the Germans for Americans.
- *September 2007*: GSG-9 raiders arrested three members of the Islamic Jihad Union with 1,500 pounds of chemicals earmarked for construction of bombs to be used against U.S. facilities in Germany.

At present, GSG-9 consists of three separate teams. The first, with 100 members, handles incidents occurring on dry land. The second, also with 100 officers, is trained for operations at sea, including hijackings of ships and oil platforms. The third, with 50 members, conducts airborne operations, including helicopter airlifts and parachute jumps. GSG-9's Central Services division maintains the unit's weapons, while a Documentation Unit handles communications and a Training Unit prepares new recruits for service.

RENEA

Albania's highly respected national SWAT team is RENEA, short for *Reparti i Neutralizimit te Elementit te Armatosur* ("Unit for the Neutralization of Armed Elements"). Created in 1991, RENEA is deployed for rescue operations (including both hostage situations and natural disasters), counterterrorist actions, and to suppress mob violence. Its membership and operations are cloaked in secrecy, but unverified Internet reports claim three officers killed and 40-plus wounded since RENEA's creation. The same sources say that RENEA hostage negotiators have peacefully resolved more than 500 out of 600 kidnap and hostage cases handled since 1991.[3] RENEA operations that can be verified include the following:

- *November 1992*: Officers provided food, shelter, and medical aid to victims of catastrophic flooding. One RENEA member, killed by criminals nine months later, single-handedly saved three victims from drowning.
- *April 1996*: A RENEA negotiator disarmed and arrested a man armed with a hand grenade who threatened a meeting of Albania's prime minister and Italy's president.
- *July 1998*: RENEA raiders captured five members of Osama bin Laden's terrorist Al-Qaeda group.
- *March 1999*: Armed felons murdered three policemen and four civilians, and then barricaded themselves inside a private home with three hostages. RENEA entered the house and killed all three gunmen, freeing their captives unharmed.
- *May 1999*: An Albanian citizen hijacked a bus with 14 passengers in Greece, collecting a $250,000 ransom before returning to Albania with his captives. During negotiations with RENEA, the kidnapper wounded one of his hostages, then was killed by a RENEA sniper.
- *February 2001*: RENEA crushed a mixed gang of Albanian and American criminals who smuggled cocaine supplied by Colombia's Medellín Cartel and the Sicilian Mafia.
- *January 2002*: RENEA broke up another drug-smuggling syndicate, seizing 2,205 pounds of pure heroin.

YAMAM

Yamam—short for *Yechida Mishtartit Meyuchedet* ("Special Police Unit")—is a division of Israel's Border Police, also known as the Unit for Counter-Terror Warfare. Its primary duties are prevention of terrorist attacks and rescue of hostages from armed kidnappers, though members also perform undercover police duties. With that in mind, since most of Israel's enemies are Muslim Arabs, all Yamam officers learn to speak Arabic and to wear clothing appropriate for infiltration of Muslim extremist groups.

Yamam's estimated 200 members are divided into various units, including a headquarters team, an intelligence team, and a unit assigned to test new weapons and tactics. Front-line officers are spread among five field units, each including members trained in the skills of forced entry, roping (climbing and rappelling), sniping, bomb disposal, and dog handling. Applicants between the ages of 21 and 28 are accepted after completing three years of service with the Israel Defense Services, but no police background is required. Those who survive rigorous entry tests and 12 months of training then take their place in active-duty units.

While Israel has suffered terrorist raids since 1948, Yamam was created after the May 1974 Ma'alot massacre, in which three Palestinian gunmen killed 26 persons, including 21 high school students, a pregnant woman, and a four-year-old child. The gunmen and an Israeli soldier died when troops stormed the occupied school.[4]

Since Yamam's work includes pre-emptive strikes against suspected terrorists, sometimes outside of Israel, many of its operations are conducted secretly and could be prosecuted as crimes in other nations. Two publicized incidents occurred in March 1988 and March 2000. The first involved a terrorist hijacking near Dimona, Israel, where three gunmen seized a busload of female employees from the Negev Nuclear Research Center. Yamam agents stormed the bus and killed all three hijackers, but not before the gunmen killed three women. In the second case, Yamam agents crushed a terrorist cell in Taibe, Israel, killing four subjects and arresting a fifth.

RAB

A relative newcomer on the SWAT scene, created in March 2004, the Rapid Action Battalion of Bangladesh draws members from the coun-

OPERATION THUNDERBOLT

On June 27, 1976, four gunmen—two Germans and two Palestinians—hijacked Air France Flight 139 en route from Athens to Paris; there were 250 people aboard. They diverted the plane to Libya and released one hostage who faked pregnancy, then flew on to Uganda's Entebbe Airport. On arrival there, four more terrorists joined the hijackers, encouraged by Uganda's dictator Idi Amin. The kidnappers demanded freedom for 53 terrorists jailed in Israel, France, West Germany, Switzerland, and Kenya, threatening death to the hostages if all were not freed by July 1. Negotiations pushed that deadline back to July 4 and secured the release of some hostages, but the gunmen kept 83 Jewish captives and 20 others, including the aircraft's full crew.

On July 3 Israeli officials ordered a rescue mission, sending four transport planes and two Boeing 707 jets to Africa. The Boeings landed in Nairobi, Kenya, while the military planes pushed on. At 1:00 A.M. on July 4 they landed at Entebbe, unloading commandos equipped with armored vehicles. Among the raiders was Lieutenant Colonel Ulrich Wegener, commander of Germany's GSG-9 team, invited to participate by Israel's top officials.

The raid was lightning swift, thus explaining its code name. Divided into strike teams with specific targets, the raiders destroyed a squadron of fighter planes to prevent airborne pursuit, refueled their transport planes, killed two Ugandan sentries, and invaded the airport terminal where hostages were confined. During the battle that ensued, Israelis killed all eight terrorists, two captives mistaken for gunmen, and an uncertain number of Ugandan soldiers. Several raiders were injured, but only one—team commander Yonatan Netanyahu—died, from a sniper's gunshot. One hostage, separated from the others at a nearby hospital, was subsequently executed on Idi Amin's orders, in retaliation for the rescue. Her body was flown back to Israel for burial in June 1979.

try's military and police. Operating on the motto "Bangladesh is My Pride," the RAB lists its tasks as including the following:

1. Internal security duties
2. Recovery of unauthorized weapons and explosives
3. Apprehension of armed criminal gangs
4. Assisting other law enforcing agencies
5. Gathering intelligence on criminal activities
6. Investigating any offense as directed by the government
7. Other duties that the government assigns from time to time[5]

Since its creation, the RAB claims credit for seizing 3,592 illegal weapons, 38,734 rounds of ammunition, and 2,580 bombs.[6] Its arrests totaled 25,632 as of April 2009, including 458 suspects who died "during exchange of fire." Those jailed included 1,303 alleged terrorists, 1,485 hijackers, 6,229 drug offenders, and 3,246 persons charged with weapons or explosives violations.[7]

Unfortunately, serious concerns exist concerning RAB's political activities. Since 2005, journalists have reported accusations of torture and summary execution lodged by government critics, citing an average weekly toll of two or three persons killed by RAB agents. Most officially die in "crossfires" between police and criminals, yet suspicion of misconduct lingers.[8] In 2008 Amnesty International logged 440,000 arbitrary arrests nationwide, with numerous reports of torture conducted by various police and military agencies.[9] Concerning the RAB, Amnesty cited the following troubling case:

> Sahebullah was reportedly detained on 16 May by Rapid Action Battalion (RAB) personnel and tortured in the office of the director of the Rajshahi Medical College Hospital. Both his legs were reportedly broken. He was arrested after demanding that a doctor attend to his wife, who had not been treated for 12 hours. She died the next day.[10]

ARGENTINA'S HAWKS

Despite a troubled history of revolution, military dictatorship, and "dirty wars" involving 30,000 deaths or disappearances, Argentina did not create a dedicated antiterrorist SWAT team until 1978.[11] That unit is the *Brigada Especial Operativa Halcón* ("Hawk Special Operations Brigade"), organized to provide security when Argentina hosted the World Cup in June 1978.

Today, the Hawk Brigade consists of 75 frontline officers, divided into five teams with 15 members each. Each team includes eight tactical assaulters, two snipers, one bomb-disposal expert, one negotiator, one medic, one communications specialist, and one intelligence officer. Before assignment to a working team, recruits must complete six months of training that includes combat shooting, sniping, handling explosives, martial arts, parachute jumping, airborne insertions by helicopter, and offensive driving.

While many of Argentina's military-police leaders faced harsh criticism and occasional prosecution for their actions during the Dirty War of 1976–83, the Hawk Brigade emerged from those violent years with a relatively clean reputation. The unit's most controversial case involves the so-called Ramallo Massacre of September 17, 1999.

In that incident, three bandits robbed a Ramallo bank on September 16, and then barricaded themselves inside until the next day, when they tried to escape by car, using hostages as human shields. Hawk Brigade officers fired on their car, killing one gunman and two hostages. Provincial governor Eduardo Duhalde blamed journalists for disrupting police negotiations. One of the surviving gunmen, Martín Saldaña, was later found hanged in his cell. Authorities called it suicide, but a 2007 report found that Saldaña was knocked unconscious and strangled, then hanged to simulate suicide. No one was ever charged with his murder.

CHINA'S WOLVES

The People's Republic of China won its bid to host the 2008 Olympic Games in July 2001. Five years later, with construction nearly finished on Beijing's Olympic Village, Chinese authorities staged a public ceremony to unveil *two* new SWAT teams on April 27, 2006. One unit, the People's Armed Police Beijing SWAT team, was placed in charge of Olympic security measures, while the other—called the Snow Wolf Commando Unit (SWCU)—shouldered a list of duties including counterterrorism, bomb disposal, anti-hijacking measures, and riot control.

(Continues on page 106)

ORIGINAL SWAT WORLD CHALLENGE

The Original SWAT World Challenge is an annual competition staged for SWAT teams representing various states and foreign countries. Launched in 2004 as the World SWAT Challenge, it was held at the training headquarters of Blackwater World-wide, a private military company based in North Carolina. Twelve teams competed in a range of challenges including a "Bushmaster High-Angle Hell," a Glock Pistol Shoot-Off, High-Risk Warrant Service, "Leupold Sniper Surprise," "Scott Masked Entry," a Range Run, a Stress Course, and Zodiac Rescue using Zodiac-brand inflatable boats. (The other challenge names also reflect specific corporate sponsors.) First-place honors in 2004 were claimed by the San Antonio (Texas) Police Department.

In April 2005 Original SWAT Footwear assumed sponsorship of the games and changed the competition's name to its present title and shifted its location to Las Vegas, Nevada. Eighteen teams participated in six events, including a Pistol Shoot-Off, "Scott Tunnel Torture," a Tactical Traverse and the Range Run, a Three-Gun Challenge, Warrant Service, and a Zodiac Attack. International participants included teams from Canada, Germany, and Jordan, with first-prize captured by Germany's GSG-9.

In 2006 the competition moved to Camp Robinson, a National Guard base near Little Rock, Arkansas, which also hosted the games in 2007–08. Participating teams—including GSG-9, a team from Taiwan, and another from Canada's Bruce Power nuclear plant—competed in eight events, including a Car Assault, LEOPARD (*Law Enforcement Officer Performance and Response Drill*) Live Fire, Masked Entry, a Pistol Shoot-Off, a Range Run, a Sniper Challenge, a Three-Gun Challenge, and a Zodiac Attack. Germany's GSG-9 group won for the second consecutive year.

In 2006 Original SWAT also assumed sponsorship of regional competitons, beginning that year with the Northeastern SWAT Challenge, followed by the Rocky Mountain Tactical

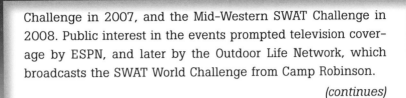

Challenge in 2007, and the Mid-Western SWAT Challenge in 2008. Public interest in the events prompted television coverage by ESPN, and later by the Outdoor Life Network, which broadcasts the SWAT World Challenge from Camp Robinson.

(continues)

Canadian SWAT team members shoot at targets during the Original SWAT World Challenge in April 2007. (*AP Photo/Mike Wintroath*)

(continued)

The SWAT World Challenge drew 28 teams in April 2007, including GSG-9, two Canadian teams, and a team from Aruba. Contestants participated in a Glock Pistol Shoot-Off, a LEOPARD Challenge, a Range Run, a "Scott Entry Problem," a Sniper Challenge, a Three-Gun Challenge, a Vehicle Assault, and a Zodiac Attack. Top honors went to the Ocean County (New Jersey) Sheriff's Department.

April 2008 brought 20 teams to Camp Robinson, with Aruba and Taiwan the foreign contestants. Events included an Assault Course, the Glock Pistol Shoot-Off, LEOPARD Live Fire, a Range Run, Run and Gun, "Simunitions Active Shooter" (using simulated-fire technology), Sniper Defense, a Three-Gun Challenge, Vehicle Assault, and Warrant Service. As in 2007, the Ocean County Sheriff's Department claimed first place.

Designed to test the fitness, organization, skills, and teamwork of competing SWAT teams, the Original SWAT World Challenge has inspired competing events, but it remains the most prestigious in the field. Its present owner, On Target Challenge, is an event management and television production company based in Maryland, which also sponsors the Firefighter Combat Challenge, the Firefighter Relay, the LEOPARD Challenge, and the Marine Corps Super Squad Challenge.

(Continued from page 103)

The SWCU took its name from the arctic wolf, a predator known for enduring harsh conditions. Much remains secret concerning the Snow Wolves, including their choice of weapons, vehicles, and other equipment, but Chinese authorities report that most recruits join the team at age 18, after serving at least one year with the People's Armed Police. That marks the Snow Wolves as the "youngest" SWAT team on Earth, but their members receive the same vigorous training as any other team worldwide.

During their April 2006 premiere exhibition, Beijing SWAT team members stormed a building for the entertainment of their audience. Snow Wolves did not participate, because their superiors feared exposure of secret equipment and methods. Two years later, SWCU members surfaced in England, guarding the Olympic torch on its passage through London.

HELSINKI'S BEARS

Finland continues the trend of naming SWAT teams after natural predators—in this case the *Karhu-ryhmä* (Bear Squad), officially known as the Readiness Unit of the Helsinki Police Department. Created soon after the 1972 Munich massacre, the Bear Squad's first public performance occurred three years later, when its officers provided security for the Organization for Security and Co-operation in Europe's annual conference in Helsinki.

The Bear Squad operates nationwide, under authority of Finland's Ministry of the Interior. Its structure includes leadership and training units, plus direction-action, technical, canine, bomb-disposal, and negotiation teams. In 2008 the Bear Squad included 90 officers, rather curiously nicknamed *Karhukopla* (Beagle Boys), after a group of roguish characters appearing in some Walt Disney comic books.

GIPN

Another SWAT team created soon after the Munich slaughter, the *Groupes d'Intervention de la Police Nationale* (French National Police Intervention Groups), began with 30 members in October 1972. According to unverified Internet reports, the GIPN reached its peak of growth with 11 separate groups, which were reduced to seven by 1985, and then increased again to nine in 1992–93. If those reports are trustworthy, 24-man teams operate in the cities of Lyon and Marseilles, while 16-man teams are based in Bordeaux, Lille, Nice, Rennes, and Strasbourg. Two overseas units also exist, on the French-owned islands of New Caledonia and Réunion.[12]

While GIPN officers are fully trained and equipped to deal with any SWAT-type emergencies, they are not alone in the field. Rival agencies

French Groupes d'Intervention de la Police Nationale (GIPN) team members participate in a training exercise involving an attack scenario with Research, Assistance, Intervention, and Deterrence (RAID) elite police teams. (*AP Photo/Jacques Brinon*)

include the National Gendarmerie Intervention Group, created in 1973 with headquarters at Satory; the Parachute Intervention Squadron of the National Gendarmerie, launched in 1984 to conduct airborne counterterrorist operations; and RAID (*Research, Assistance, Intervention, Deterrence*), nicknamed the "Black Panthers," organized in 1985 to prevent terrorist attacks on aircraft, trains, nuclear plants, and other strategic sites. While all of these groups operate behind a cloak of secrecy, the National Gendarmerie Intervention Group claims more than 1,000 successful operations, with over 1,000 arrests, 500 hostages rescued, and a dozen terrorists killed.[13]

Chronology

1964	New Zealand Police leaders create a Special Tactics Group
1965	Toronto's police department establishes an Emergency Task Force
1967	LAPD launches the first recognized American SWAT team
1969	**December 8:** LAPD SWAT conducts its first major raid against the Black Panthers
1971	Creation of the U.S. Marshals Service Special Operations Group (SOG)
1972	**September 5:** A terrorist attack on the Olympic Games in Munich, Germany, prompts creation of SWAT teams throughout Europe
	October–December: New SWAT teams include Austria's EKO Cobra squad, Denmark's AKS team, Finland's Bear Unit, and two French teams, the GIGN and GIPN
1973	FBI SWAT teams organize in response to the Wounded Knee incident
	February 27: Native American activists occupy the town of Wounded Knee, South Dakota, beginning a siege by SOG officers that lasts until May 5
	April: Germany's Federal Police create the GSG-9 SWAT team
1974	New SWAT teams include the DEA's Mobile Enforcement Team, Belgium's Federal Police Special Units, Israel's Yamam team, and Italy's Central Security Operations Service

	May 17: LAPD SWAT battles the Symbionese Liberation Army
1975	**July:** Hong Kong police organize a Special Duties Unit Queensland, Australia, creates the Special Emergency Response Team
1976	Police in Oslo, Norway, form the Delta SWAT team
1977	New SWAT units include Japan's Special Assault Team and the Special Operations Group based in Victoria, Australia
	October 18: GSG 9 officers storm a hijacked airliner in Mogadishu, Somalia, rescuing 84 hostages and killing four terrorists
	November 21: The U.S. Army creates Delta Force to combat terrorism
1978	New SWAT teams include Brazil's Special Police Operations Battalion; the Greek Special Anti-Terrorist Unit; Ireland's Emergency Response Unit; Italy's Special Intervention Group; Spain's Special Operations Group; the Hawk Special Operations Brigade in Buenos Aires, Argentina; South Australia's STAR Force; Serbia's Special Anti-Terrorist Unit; Tasmania's Special Operations Group; and Western Australia's Tactical Response Group
1979	Russia creates the OMON Special Purpose Police Squad, while the Swedish Police Service establishes the Piketen task force
1980	**August:** The U.S. Navy creates SEAL Team 6 for counterterrorist action
1981	Norway's army organizes the FSK special forces unit to combat terrorism
1982	The FBI creates a mobile Hostage Rescue Team (HRT)
	October: Iceland organizes the Viking Squad SWAT team
1983	Sri Lanka Police leaders create a counterterrorist Special Task Force
	May: The Philippine National Police Special Action Force begins operations

1984	Creation of the U.S. Border Patrol's Patrol Tactical Unit
	July 18: San Diego SWAT officers kill deranged gunman James Huberty
	December 8: Neo-Nazi terrorist Robert Mathews dies in a shootout with FBI SWAT officers on Whidbey Island in Puget Sound, north of Seattle, Washington
1985	New SWAT teams include India's National Security Guards, Taiwan's "Thunder Squad," and the French RAID unit
1987	**November 21 to December 4:** Inmate riots prompt the Federal Bureau of Prisons to create Special Operations and Response Teams
1991	New SWAT teams include Albania's RENEA unit, Brazil's Special Operations Group, and the State Protection Group of New South Wales, Australia
1992	**August 21:** Following the murder of an SOG officer, FBI-HRT units begin a 12-day siege of Randy Weaver's home at Ruby Ridge, Idaho
1993	New SWAT units include the Royal Canadian Mounted Police Emergency Response Team and Singapore's STAR squad
	February 28 to April 19: The Branch Davidian siege at Waco, Texas, claims the lives of four ATF officers and 76 civilians
1994	Creation of Argentina's Federal Operations Special Group
1996	Creation of Holland's Special Intervention Service
	March 25 to June 13: Montana Freemen sieged by SOG officers
1997	Creation of Malaysia's PGK SWAT team and the ZUZ unit of German Customs
2003	**May:** Serbia's Ministry of Internal Affairs creates the PTJ antiterror unit
	July: Australia's Northern Territory creates the Territory Response Group
2004	**March 26:** Bangladesh organizes an antiterrorist Rapid Action Battalion

	May: First SWAT World Challenge competition held in North Carolina
2006	British Columbia creates the Municipal Integrated Emergency Response Team
	April 27: Creation of Beijing's Snow Wolf Commando Unit
2008	**February 6:** Randal Simmons becomes the first LAPD SWAT officer killed on duty
2009	**March 21:** Two Oakland, California, SWAT officers die in a shootout with fugitive cop-killer Lovelle Mixon

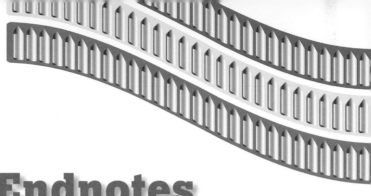

Endnotes

Introduction

1. "America's most dangerous jobs," CNN, http://money.cnn.com/2007/08/07/pf/2006_most_dangerous_jobs/index.htm (Accessed June 24, 2010).
2. Officer Down Memorial Page, http://www.odmp.org (Accessed May 19, 2010).

Chapter 1

1. Grand Jury Report: Investigation of Missing Guerra Files (September 2004), http://media.mnginteractive.com/media/paper36/Columbine_Grand_Jury_Report.pdf (Accessed May 19, 2010).
2. Robert Snow, *SWAT Teams* (New York: Da Capo Press, 2000), 49.
3. Jessica Gresko, "20 years later, San Ysidro McDonald's massacre remembered," *North County Times* (Escondido, Calif.), July 17, 2004.
4. LAPD, "Challenges Faced by S.W.A.T.," http://www.lapdonline.org/metropolitan_division/content_basic_view/850 (Accessed May 19, 2010).
5. Hans Halberstadt, *SWAT Team* (Osceola, Wis.: Motorbooks International, 1994), 32.
6. Halberstadt, 33-34.
7. Scott Buhrmaster, "Suicide By Cop: 15 warning signs that you might be involved," http://www.policeone.com/suicide-by-cop/articles/84176-Suicide-By-Cop-15-warning-signs-that-you-might-be-involved (Accessed May 19, 2010).
8. Richard Parent, "Aspects of Police Use of Deadly Force in North America: The Phenomenon Of Victim-Precipitated Homicide" (Ph.D. diss., Simon Fraser University, Burnaby, B.C., 2004.)
9. Amy Rippel, "Fla. man killed by deputies predicted his own death," *South Florida Sun-Sentinel,* May 27, 2005.
10. "LAPD officers kill man who shot at them while holding baby," Associated Press, July 10, 2005; "Toddler and father killed by police," http://www.workers.org/2005/us/ lapd-0728 (Accessed May 19, 2010).
11. Gary Taylor, "Deputies shoot 8th grade student on school campus," *Orlando Sentinel,* January 13, 2006.
12. Orange County Sheriff's Department, "SWAT Tryouts Test Applicants for Skills, Strengths and Fears," http://blog.ocsd.org/post/2008/04/30/SWAT-Tryouts-Test-Law-Enforcement-Skills-and-Personal-Best.aspx (Accessed May 19, 2010).
13. Ibid.
14. Ibid.

Chapter 2

1. Dennis Roddy and Sadie Gurman, "Pa. SWAT marksman 'justified' in shooting standoff suspect who had 2 guns," *Pittsburgh Post-Gazette,* January 10, 2009.
2. Ibid.
3. "Pullman: SWAT team called in to search WSU fraternity," *Moscow-Pullman* (Wash.) *Daily News,* January 22, 2009.
4. J.D. Tuccille, "SWAT raid for underage drinking at Washington State University," *Civil Liberties Examiner*, January 26, 2009.
5. "Pullman: SWAT team called in to search WSU fraternity."
6. "Three arrested in SWAT raid," *Times Record News* (Wichita Falls, Texas), February 3, 2009.
7. "ESD-ESU," Police N.Y., http://www.policeny.com/esdtrucks1.html (Accessed May 14, 2010).
8. Snow, *SWAT Teams,* 274
9. "SWAT Team," http://www.nationmaster.com/encyclopedia/SWAT-team (Accessed May 19, 2010).
10. Marlee Macleod, "Charles Whitman: The Texas Tower Sniper," Crime Library, http://www.trutv.com/library/crime/notorious_murders/mass/whitman/index_1.html (Accessed May 19, 2010).
11. Ibid.
12. Mark Gaddo, "Hell Comes to Bath," Crime Library, http://www.trutv.com/library/ crime/serial_killers/history/bath/index_1.html (Accessed May 19, 2010).
13. Radley Balko, *Overkill: The Rise of Paramilitary Police Raids in America* (Washington, D.C.: Cato Institute, 2006), 1.
14. U.S. Census Bureau, http://www.census.gov/main/www/cen2000.html (Accessed May 19, 2010).
15. Balko, 9.
16. Amy Goldstein, "The private arm of the law," *Washington Post,* January 2, 2007.
17. Dennis Hevesi, "Standoff at U.N. with a protester," *New York Times,* April 12, 1992.
18. Balko, 8.
19. Ibid.

Chapter 3

1. Jason Kandel, "SWAT officer killed in Winnetka standoff," *Los Angeles Daily News,* February 8, 2008.
2. "5 dead after 12-hour standoff at a San Fernando Valley home," *Los Angeles Times,* February 8, 2008.
3. LAPD, "History of S.W.A.T.," http://www.lapdonline.org/metropolitan_division/content_basic_view/849 (Accessed May 19, 2010); "Darryl F. Gates," Nation Master, http://www.nationmaster.com/encyclopedia/Darryl-F.-Gates (Accessed May 19, 2010).
4. Michael Newton, *Bitter Grain: The Story of the Black Panther Party* (Los Angeles: Holloway House, 1980), 100–102.
5. Internet Movie Database, http://www.imdb.com/title/tt0062539/episodes; "Jack Webb," http://www.spiritus-temporis.com/jack-webb (Accessed May 19, 2010).
6. Ex-Liberal in Hollywood, http://exlibhollywood.blogspot.com/2008/03/lapd-swat-scandal-grows.html (Accessed May 19, 2010).
7. The Symbionese Federation, http://www.feastofhateandfear.com/archives/sla.html (Accessed May 19, 2010).
8. LAPD, *The Symbionese Liberation Army in Los Angeles* (July 19, 1974).

9. Jack Dunphy, "Unstoppable," *National Review Online* (December 8, 2006), http://article.nationalreview.com/300497/unstoppable/jack-dunphy (Accessed May 19, 2010).

10. LAPD, "Heroic measures save LAPD officer's life," http://www.lapdonline.org/june_ 2006/news_view/32535; Golden Badge Foundation, http://www.goldenbadgefoundation.org/2007heroism.php (Accessed May 19, 2010).

11. Internet Movie Database, http://www.imdb.com/find?s=tt&q=swat (Accessed May 19, 2010).

12. CNN, "Botched L.A. bank heist turns into bloody shootout," http://www.cnn.com/US/9702/28/shootout.update/ (Accessed June 24, 2010).

13. "Botched L.A. bank heist turns into bloody shootout."

14. "Family of robber killed in L.A. shootout sues," CNN, April 12, 1997; "Mistrial declared in case stemming from shootout," *New York Times,* March 17, 2000.

15. Joel Rubin, "SWAT to get female trainee," *Los Angeles Times,* March 29, 2008.

16. Ibid.

17. Ibid.

18. Ibid.

19. Robert Perry, "Memo to NPR: Fact checking is a wonderful thing," *Los Angeles Daily News,* April 30, 2008.

20. LAPD Wife, http://www.lapdwife.com/2008/04/women-and-swat.html (Accessed May 19, 2010).

21. Ibid.

22. LAPD, "LAPD releases board of inquiry summary of SWAT team analysis," http://lapdblog.typepad.com/lapd_blog/2008/04/lapd-releases-b.html (Accessed May 19, 2010).

23. "Report released on LAPD SWAT unit," KNBC-TV, Channel 4 (Los Angeles), April 16, 2008.

24. Ibid.

Chapter 4

1. Dan Benson, "FBI agent killed in training devoted life to public safety," *Milwaukee Journal Sentinel,* December 16, 2006.

2. Ibid.

3. FBI, Hall of Honor, http://www.fbi.gov/libref/hallhonor/hallhonor.htm (Accessed May 19, 2010).

4. Benson.

5. FBI, Hall of Honor.

6. FBI, Critical Incident Response Group, http://www.fbi.gov/hq/isd/cirg/tact.htm (Accessed July 27, 2010).

7. FBI, Critical Incident Response Group.

8. Brent Smith, *Terrorism in America: Pipe Bombs and Pipe Dreams* (Albany: State University of New York Press, 1994), 73–76.

9. Smith, 66.

10. Firearms Tactical Institute, Tactical Briefs No. 7 (July 1998), http://www.firearms tactical.com/briefs7.htm (Accessed May 19, 2010).

11. David Lohr, "Randy Weaver: Siege at Ruby Ridge," Crime Library, http://www.trutv.com/library/crime/gangsters_outlaws/cops_others/randy_weaver/1.html (Accessed May 19, 2010).

12. Ibid.

13. FBI, Critical Incident Response Group.

14. U.S. Department of Justice, "Three inmates' conspiracy and extortion scheme to seize the property of federal prison officials results in

additional 14–15 years in prison" (April 7, 2008), http://oklahomacity.fbi.gov/dojpressrel/pressrel08/apr7_08.htm (Accessed May 19, 2010).

15. FBI, Critical Incident Response Group.

16. Office of the Inspector General, The Federal Bureau of Investigation's Efforts to Protect the Nation's Seaports (March 2006), http://www.justice.gov/oig/reports/FBI/a0626/findings2.htm (Accessed May 19, 2010).

17. Ibid.

18. Ibid.

Chapter 5

1. Kevin Vaughan, "Denver cops aren't buying exotic crowd-control weapons for DNC," *Rocky Mountain News*, July 24, 2008.

2. Southern Poverty Law Center, "Skinheads arrested in plot to kill Obama," http://www.splcenter.org/blog/2008/10/27/skinheads-arrested-in-plot-to-kill-obama (Accessed May 19, 2010).

3. "Man is arrested in Obama threat," *New York Times*, January 16, 2009.

4. Less Lethal Working Group, http://www.less-lethal.org/web/home.aspx (Accessed May 19, 2010).

5. Halberstadt, 86.

6. National Institute of Justice, http://www.ojp.usdoj.gov/nij/topics/technology/body-armor/welcome.htm (Accessed May 19, 2010).

7. NIJ, *Ballistic Resistance of Body Armor*, http://www.ncjrs.gov/pdffiles1/nij/223054. pdf, 3–5 (Accessed May 19, 2010).

8. "The Battle of People's Park," *Rolling Stone* (June 14, 1969), http://www.beauty-reality.com/travel/

travel/sanFran/peoplespark3.html (Accessed May 19, 2010).

9. Ian MacKinnon, "RUC reopens case of boy killed by plastic bullet," *The Independent* (London), August 24, 1995; "Plastic bullets on way out," United Press International, July 24, 2001; Emma Ross, "Study: Rubber bullets dangerous," Associated Press, May 24, 2002.

10. ACLU, *Pepper Spray Update: More Fatalities, More Questions* (June 1995), http://www.aclu-sc.org/attach/p/Pepper_Spray_New_Questions.pdf (Accessed May 19, 2010).

11. H. Salem, E.J. Olajos, L.L. Miller, and S.A. Thompson, *Capsaicin Toxicology Review*, (U.S. Army Engineer Research and Development Center, Life Science Department, 1993), 4.

12. Halberstadt, 109–121.

13. Halberstadt, *SWAT Team,* 9, 47, 61-62.

14. Halberstadt, 76, 84–85.

15. Halberstadt, 62.

16. Halberstadt, 62–63.

17. Halberstadt, 63–64.

18. Halberstadt, 64.

19. Lenco Armored Vehicles, http://www.swattrucks.com (Accessed May 19, 2010).

Chapter 6

1. Thomas Hunter, "Operation Nimrod: The SAS assault at Princes Gate," http://www.angelfire.com/wa/cagiva2/nimrod.html (Accessed May 19, 2010).

2. Edward F. Mickolus, *Transnational Terrorism,* (Westport, Conn.: Greenwood Press, 1980), 3–4.

3. Mickolus, 570–573.

4. John Dunlop, "The October 2022 Moscow hostage-taking incident,"

Radio Free Europe, December 18, 2003; "Families claim death toll from gas in Moscow siege kept secret," *The Guardian* (London), October 18, 2003.

5. Andrew Osborn, "Beslan siege investigation chief points finger," *The Independent* (London), December 29, 2005.

6. Ed Grabianowski, "How hostage negotiation works," http://people.howstuffworks. com/hostage-negotiation2.htm (Accessed May 19, 2010).

7. Ibid.

8. Ibid.

9. Ibid.

10. Magnus Ranstorp, *Hizb'allah in Lebanon: The Politics of the Western Hostage Crisis* (New York, St. Martin's Press, 1997), 95; "US 'seeks justice' for hijacker," BBC News, December 20, 2005; "Bomb kills Hezbollah militant wanted by U.S.," NBC News, February 13, 2008.

11. Public Agency Training Council, http://www.patc.com/courses/hostage-negotiationsphaseI.shtml; Midwest Police Consultants, http://www.midwestpolice.com/ index.php/upcoming-training/67-crisis-hostage-negotiation-level-ii-intermediate (Accessed May 19, 2010).

Chapter 7

1. Tom Jackman, "Va. officer might be suspended for fatality," *Washington Post,* November 25, 2006.

2. "A tragedy of errors," *Washington Post,* January 20, 2007.

3. Jackman.

4. Cato Institute, http://www.cato.org/about.php (Accessed May 19, 2010).

5. "Nose to nose," *Time* (August 14, 1978), http://www.time.com/time/magazine/ article/0,9171,946962,00.html (Accessed May 19, 2010); "Surrender immediately," *Time* (August 21, 1978), http://www.time.com/time/magazine/article/0,9171,919800,00.html (Accessed May 19, 2010).

6. William K. Stevens, "Police drop bomb on radicals' home in Philadelphia," *New York Times,* May 14, 1985; Robert Hanley, "After the inferno, tears and bewilderment," *New York Times,* May 15, 1985.

7. "Philadelphia, city officials ordered to pay $1.5 Million to MOVE survivor," CNN, June 24, 1996.

8. Radley Balko, *Overkill: The Rise of Paramilitary Police Raids in America* (Washington, D.C.: The Cato Institute, 2006), 1.

9. Balko, 7.

10. S.K. Bardwell, "New evidence surfaces in flawed SWAT drug raid," *Houston Chronicle,* June 5, 1994; Jennifer Liebrum, "Life imprisonment for convicted killer; Man found guilty in death of officer," *Houston Chronicle,* September 23, 1994.

11. Leigh Dyer, "Anatomy of a deadly SWAT raid," *Charlotte Observer,* September 9, 1998.

12. Joshua Good, "Fulton woman slain during drug raid," *Atlanta Journal-Constitution,* September 23, 2000.

13. House of Representatives, *Investigation into the Activities of Federal Law Enforcement Agencies Toward the Branch Davidians, 13th Report, Section 4* (August 2, 1996), http://en.wikisource.org/wiki/Activities_of_Federal_Law_Enforcement_Agencies_Toward_the_Branch_Davidians (Accessed May 19, 2010).

14. House of Representatives, *Investigation into the Activities of Federal Law Enforcement Agencies Toward the Branch Davidians, 13th Report,* Section 8.

15. Larry King, "Man shot in apartment by police hopes for justice," *Philadelphia Inquirer,* April 7, 2004; "Pennsylvania Police Fail To Investigate Shooting of Unarmed Man," Associated Press, September 3, 2004.

16. Joseph M. Giordano, "Woman is shot, killed by police in drug raid," *Dundalk* (Md.) *Eagle,* January 27, 2005; Joseph M. Giordano, "Petition reflects anguish," *Dundalk Eagle,* March 31, 2005.

17. Kathy Jefcoats, "Henry police raid 'inexcusable'; Couple gets wake-up call meant for their neighbor," *Atlanta Journal-Constitution,* October 6, 2005; Kathy Jefcoats, "Suit threatened in raid 'mistake,'" *Atlanta Journal-Constitution,* March 4, 2006.

18. Phillip Ramati and Joe Kovac Jr., "'It just went wrong,' sheriff says of slaying," *Macon Telegraph,* April 5, 2006.

19. "Minn. man shoots cops after SWAT team kicks down wrong door," *USA Today,* December 22, 2007.

20. Balko, 44–46.

Chapter 8

1. Francie Grace, "Munich massacre remembered," CBS News, September 5, 2002.

2. "Elite German force chief may visit to discuss NSG training,"

The Daily Indian, January 22, 2009.

3. "Albania," http://www.special operations.com/Foreign/Albania/Default.htm, (Accessed June 24, 2010).

4. "Ma'alot massacre," http://enc.slider.com/Enc/Ma'alot_massacre (Accessed May 19, 2010).

5. RAB Web site, http://www.rab.gov.bd/about_us.php?page=3 (Accessed May 19, 2010).

6. RAB Web site, http://www.rab.gov.bd/achievement.php?cid=4 (Accessed May 19, 2010).

7. RAB Web site, http://www.rab.gov.bd/achievement.php?cid=3 (Accessed May 19, 2010).

8. Roland Buerk, "Bangladesh's feared elite police," BBC News, December 13, 2005.

9. *Bangladesh–Amnesty International Report 2008,* http://www.amnesty.org/en/region/ bangladesh/report-2008 (Accessed May 19, 2010).

10. Ibid.

11. The Lesser Unpleasantries of the Twentieth Century, http://users.erols.com/ mwhite28/warstat5.htm#Argentina (Accessed June 24, 2010).

12. "RAID—Recherche Assistance Intervention Dissuasion," RAID, http://le.raid.free.fr/accueil.htm (Accessed May 19, 2010).

13. *Groupe d'Intervention de la Gendarmerie Nationale,* http://www.specialoperations. com/Foreign/France/GIGN/default.htm (Accessed May 19, 2010).

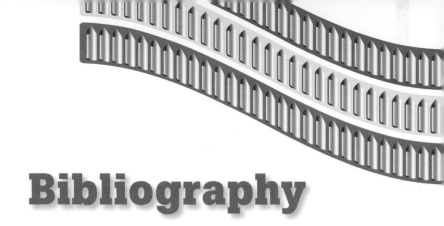

Bibliography

Coulson, Danny, and Elaine Shannon. *No Heroes: Inside the FBI's Secret Counter-Terror Force.* New York: Pocket Books, 1999.

Halberstadt, Hans. *SWAT Team: Police Special Weapons and Tactics.* Osceola, Wis.: Motorbooks International, 1994.

Holm, Michael. *SWAT Team Development and Deployment.* Shawnee Mission, Kan.: Varro Press, 2002.

Kolman, John. *The Trials and Tribulations of Becoming a SWAT Commander.* Springfield, Ill.: Charles C. Thomas, 2004.

Lonsdale, Mark. *Raids: A Tactical Guide to High Risk Warrant Service.* Los Angeles: Specialized Tactical Training Unit, 2005.

Snow, Robert. *SWAT Teams: Explosive Face-Offs with America's Deadliest Criminals.* New York: Da Capo Press, 1999.

Whitcomb, Christopher. *Cold Zero: Inside the FBI Hostage Rescue Team.* New York: Little, Brown, 2001.

Further Resources

Print

Cascio, Pat, and John McSweeny. *SWAT Battle Tactics: How to Organize, Train, and Equip a SWAT Team for Law Enforcement or Self-Defense.* Boulder, Colo.: Paladin Press, 1996. This volume details the various steps in the creation and training of a modern SWAT team for all manners of crises.

Haynes, Richard. *The SWAT Cyclopedia: A Handy Desk Reference of Terms, Techniques, and Strategies Associated With the Police Special Weapons and Tactics Function.* Springfield, Ill.: Charles C. Thomas, 1999. Haynes provides a comprehensive dictionary of terms related to SWAT team equipment, training, and tactical operations.

Thompson, Leroy. *Hostage Rescue Manual: Tactics of the Counter-Terrorist Professionals.* Newbury, England: Greenhill Books, 2006. This manual focuses specifically on hostage-rescue techniques for SWAT negotiators and tactical officers in the modern age of terrorism.

Online

North American SWAT Training Association
http://www.nasta.ws
The NASTA Web site profiles one of America's leading organizations dedicated to the training of SWAT team leaders and officers.

World SWAT Challenge Series
http://www.swatseries.com
This site provides the history and details of the World Series of SWAT competition, open to American and international teams.

The Officer Down Memorial Page
http://www.odmp.org
The Officer Down site offers case histories of all known American police officers killed in the line of duty, including SWAT team members.

Index

About the Author

Michael Newton has published 229 books since 1977, with 18 forth-coming from various houses through 2011. His history of the Florida Ku Klux Klan (*The Invisible Empire,* 2001) won the Florida Historical Society's 2002 Rembert Patrick Award for "Best Book in Florida History," and his *Encyclopedia of Cryptozoology* was one of the American Library Association's Outstanding Reference Works in 2006. His non-fiction work includes numerous volumes for Chelsea House Publishers and Facts On File.

DATE DUE